What will your life be like?

What will your life be like next year?

Five years from now?

The answer to that question will not

be determined primarily by chance,

your DNA or by the state of the economy.

It will not be your appearance, talent,

family of origin or your education

that will most shape your destiny.

The best predictor of your future

is the vitality of your faith."

Steve Cordle

Hear it

See it

Risk it

How Faith Grows

By Steve Cordle

Market
Square
BOOKS

Hear it, See it, Risk it

How Faith Grows

By Steve Cordle

©2019 Steve Cordle
books@marketsquarebooks.com
P.O. Box 23664 Knoxville, Tennessee 37933

ISBN: 978-1-7323092-5-8

Library of Congress: 2019931448

Printed and Bound in the United States of America

Editor: Kristin Lighter
Cover Illustration by Jason Klanderud

Table of Contents

Introduction 1

Part One: Your Faith Can Grow

Chapter 1: How Faith Grows 8

Chapter 2: Hear it 19

Chapter 3: See it 32

Chapter 4: Risk it 45

Part Two: Defending Our Faith

Chapter 5: Troubleshooting 58

Chapter 6: Doubt – Spiritual Hearing Loss 61

Chapter 7: Fear – A Failure of Imagination 75

Chapter 8: Sin – A Step in the Wrong Direction 91

Chapter 9: Pain – Faith's Defining Moment 102

Part Three: Living It

Chapter 10: Takes a Community 114

Chapter 11: Know it 127

Chapter 12: With Heart and Mind 138

Conclusion 149

Acknowledgments 151

[Handwritten margin notes:]
July 10th — bracketing Chapters 2–4
July 24th — bracketing Chapters 5–7
Aug 7 — bracketing Chapters 8–9
Aug 21 — bracketing Chapters 10–11
Sept 4 — bracketing Chapter 12 and Conclusion

Introduction

"... According to your faith let it be done to you."

— Jesus

Matthew 9:29 (NIV)

It was time to decide. I sat alone in an overstuffed chair in the quiet vacation cabin as my wife and children enjoyed the nearby lake. For eighteen months I had been trying to discern whether or not God was calling me to start a new church. I had prayed for guidance. I had studied everything I could find about church planting (which wasn't much in 1990). I had talked to every church planter I knew (again, not many). Now, it was decision time; should I start a new church or not?

I asked myself the classic question, "What would you attempt if you knew you couldn't fail?" I knew my answer immediately: I would start a new church that reached unreached people. Just then, an image flashed through my mind's eye. I saw myself standing on the platform of what I assumed was a new church. It looked much different than the traditional chancel of the church I was serving at the time.

I asked myself a follow-up question, "So, why don't you do it?"

"Because I might fail," I replied to me. I was not sure how I would handle that emotionally and spiritually.

Realizing I was at a crucial juncture, I challenged myself. "So, are you going to live out of fear or faith?" There could be only one answer. In spite of my doubts and insecurities, I knew I could not let fear guide me. My decision was made. I returned home and wrote a proposal for a new church start and submitted it to my

1

denomination. At that time, there was very little precedent (and some suspicion) for that sort of initiative, and I was unsure of how it would be received. Nonetheless, the leadership approved it, and a few months later Crossroads Church was born.

Over the last twenty-five years, thousands of lives have been changed by the power of God through Crossroads Church, including mine. The experience of starting a church with no people and see it grow to five campuses in two states has both strengthened and challenged my faith. There have been seasons my confidence in God soared as we saw remarkable answers to prayer and multiple 'only God' moments. At other times, I felt my faith buckling under pressure and pain that I did not see coming. Today, as the journey continues, I am deeply grateful for the unreasonably rich blessings God has let me experience. It all started with a simple step of faith that day in the cabin.

According to Your Faith

What will your life be like next year? Five years from now? The answer to that question will not be determined primarily by chance, your DNA or by the state of the economy. It will not be your appearance, talent, family of origin or your education that will most shape your destiny. The best predictor of your future is the vitality of your faith.

The level of your faith will influence the type of challenges to which you will rise and the attitudes you will display. It will govern the amount of resilience you will show in the face of hardship, the depth of your relationships and the amount of God's power that flows through your life. Your faith will even determine whether or not you live beyond the grave. Our faith shapes more of our lives than we realize.

One day two blind men heard that Jesus was passing through their area and they seized the opportunity to meet him. Matthew 9 says,

> As Jesus went on from there, two blind men followed him, calling out, "Have mercy on us, Son of David!"
> When he had gone indoors, the blind men came to him, and he asked them, "Do you believe that I am able to do this?"

2

"Yes, Lord," they replied.

Then he touched their eyes and said, **"According to your faith let it be done to you"; and their sight was restored.**[1]

These two men had learned to cope with their blindness, but they yearned for more. They wanted to see! And because of their faith, they did. It was their faith that prompted them to call out to Jesus. They followed Jesus into that home because they were convinced that he could make them see. When Jesus asked them if they believed he could heal them, faith led them to answer, "yes." As a result, they received their sight and their lives were transformed.

"According to your faith let it be done to you." That statement is inspiring if we are confident in our faith. But if our faith feels shaky or uncertain, Jesus' words can sound de-motivating instead of encouraging. The good news is no matter how solid or wobbly your faith is today, your faith can grow.

Years ago, when my eldest son was learning to ride a bicycle, I ran alongside him to prevent him from tipping over. That lasted for about one day. After that, I bought him some training wheels. Those external props provided stability as he learned how to balance, pedal and steer. When I saw him maneuvering confidently, I removed the training wheels. Now an adult, he recently completed a 150-mile bike ride, finishing with one of the best times out of the group of 400 riders. The training wheels worked!

Think of this book as "training wheels" for your faith. It breaks down essential components of faith into a simple biblically-sourced process that, when followed, results in a deeper trust in God. When our faith seems wobbly and insufficient for what we are facing, we can strengthen our faith by deliberately employing this biblical pattern. You may not always feel the need for systematically applying these steps. There will be seasons you are confident and cruising freely in your faith. Trust in God comes naturally then because, whether you realize it or not, you are following this process almost without thinking.

---

1 Matthew 9:27-30

Faith for More

This book is not about getting whatever you want by using faith to manipulate God. That is selfishness covered with a thin veneer of spirituality. Rather, this book is about how we learn to trust God more deeply, and in the process receive more of what God has always intended and promised to us. That is not an empty motivational slogan; it is a truth rooted in the message of the Scriptures.

Part One of this book is drawn from Hebrews 11, which is sometimes called the Bible's "Hall of Faith." The writer challenges us to grow in our faith by following the examples of biblical heroes. As Hebrews 6:12 says, we are to "imitate those who through faith and patience inherit what has been promised." This book is about how to do that.

The people named in Hebrews 11 were far from perfect, but because of their faith they became part of God's story and received what God promised them. Hebrews 11:33-35 reminds us:

> "... **through faith** [they] conquered kingdoms, administered justice, and gained what was promised; who shut the mouths of lions, quenched the fury of the flames, and escaped the edge of the sword; whose weakness was turned to strength; and who became powerful in battle and routed foreign armies. Women received back their dead, raised to life again. There were others who were tortured, refusing to be released so that they might gain an even better resurrection."

Conquering kingdoms, routing armies, raising the dead — that is an impressive resume for the life-changing power of faith.

The Bible also tells us that through faith:

- we enter a relationship with God and live eternally (Ephesians 2:8-9)

- we are assured we are forgiven and accepted by God (Hebrews 10:22)

- our faith-filled prayer changes circumstances (James 5:16)

- we see God's power at work in amazing ways (Mark 11:22-24)
- we are able to please God with our lives (Hebrews 11:6).

Faith motivates us to bold obedience and acts of love. More faith means less fear. Faith permits God to work through us to accomplish things far beyond our natural ability.

Part Two of this book will identify common forces which weaken our faith and provide strategies for neutralizing them. Part Three will highlight the role of community in sustaining a authentic saving faith.

The blessings for which I am most thankful are not the fruit of a magnetic personality, strategic connections, innate abilities or of my stunning good looks (irony alert). They are by-products of faith. I am certainly not implying that I am a superstar of faith — far from it. I am not a courageous person by nature. I love security. Doubt comes more naturally to me than belief. I have had my struggles with anxiety. Here's my point: if a quiet, security-loving guy like me can see God do supernatural things through faith, so can you. Really.

You may not need to defeat an attacking army, but you might be facing a battle of another kind. You might not be seeking to raise someone from the dead physically, but what if your dead hopes and dreams could be resurrected? What if your future was shaped more by faith and less by doubt or habit? Perhaps you would like less fear and more of God's power flowing through your life. You might desire more confidence that you are forgiven and that you have eternal life. If so, read on.

Ultimately it is God who initiates our faith, so there will always be some mystery surrounding how exactly faith is born and grows in us. We are not in complete control of the process. Our understanding of it will always be partial.

At the same time, it is clear that we have a role to play in becoming people of faith. After all, why would the Bible challenge us to demonstrate faith if there was nothing we could do about whether we have it or not? Why would Jesus urge his followers to "have faith in God"[2] if they either had it or they didn't? Faith grows as a cooperative effort between God and us. God will call us to faith; our role is to put ourselves in a posture to let it develop in us. Faith is like a muscle. The more you use it, the more it grows. Let the workout begin.

---

2 Mark 11:22; Matthew 21:21

Part One

Your Faith Can Grow

CHAPTER ONE
How Faith Grows

Now faith is confidence in what we hope for and
assurance about what we do not see.

Hebrews 11:1

Faith is not belief without proof, but trust without reservations – trust
in a God who has shown himself worthy of that trust.

- Alister McGrath

Brandon did not wrestle with worry - he was consumed by it. A couple of years earlier his father had contracted kidney cancer, and now Brandon was afraid that someday he would get the disease, too. Low-grade anxiety clung to him every waking moment, draining the joy out of his life. One day, weary of his constant inner struggle, he decided to confide in one of his best friends. When Brandon revealed that he was battling fear, his friend blurted out, "You're a Christian; have some faith!" Stung, Brandon walked away dejected and still mired in his anxiety. He conceded to himself that more faith would probably help. But he had no idea how, or even if, his faith could grow.

An Elusive Target

Most of us would admit there are moments we would like less doubt and more confidence in God. We want a stronger and deeper faith, one that will empower us to deal with life's difficulties and to follow Jesus boldly. Still, fewer of us know exactly what to do to develop that faith.

"Have faith!" Have you ever heard that? Maybe you have told yourself that. The question is: exactly how do I "have faith?" If you tell me to read the Bible, I know I am to open the book and start reading it. If you tell me to love my next-door neighbor, I might be able to come up with at least a few ideas of how to do that, even if they are not always easy to put into practice. If you tell me to pray, I understand what to do. But exactly what am I being told to do when I'm exhorted to "have faith?" Am I supposed to sit in a church and work up a certain spiritual feeling? Am I supposed to ignore the questions that are bombarding my mind? Exactly how do I go about having more faith?

It would be great if our faith grew deeper simply by us desiring it enough. Unfortunately, it does not. We can want a deeper faith than the one we have. More religious activity is not the answer, either. It is possible to attend more worship services, pray longer, serve others more frequently and still not move the needle on our faith level. Spiritual disciplines are vital to our spiritual health, but they do not automatically increase our trust in God, either. We engage in them with the level of faith we bring to them. For example, Brandon could study the Bible diligently and learn more of God's truth, yet remain paralyzed by anxiety over the prospect of getting cancer. He could serve others sacrificially and still doubt that God cares about the details of his life.

Desiring to grow in faith without knowing how to do it is frustrating. It can be like yearning to lose weight and using every tactic we know, only to step on the scale and see no change. That is demoralizing. Without a clear pathway to grow in faith, many Christians have concluded their faith level is like their eye color — there is nothing they can do to change it. You either have faith or you don't. As a result, they resign themselves to living at a lower level of trust in God than is necessary. If a deeper faith has seemed out of reach for you, here is some good news: you do have faith, and your faith in God can grow.

You've Got Faith

You have faith. I am confident of this because everyone has faith. Whether we are long-time followers of Christ, avowed atheists, confirmed skeptics, or questioning seekers, we each exhibit faith every day. Not everyone has faith in God, but each of us has faith. That is because faith is acting on what is unseen, and we each do that routinely.

Here is how Hebrews defines faith: "Now faith is confidence in what we hope for and assurance about what we do not see" (Hebrews 11:1 NIV).

If faith is a confident assurance and trust in what we do not see, then we each demonstrate faith daily because we must operate out of trust in big and small ways. For example, the last time you ate in a restaurant, did you demand to watch the server test your food for contaminants? Probably not. You may not have thought of eating out as an act of faith, but it is. You demonstrated faith in food preparers that you could not see. It takes faith to get behind the wheel of a car and drive to work. No one gives us a guarantee that the brakes won't fail or that the steering column will not malfunction. Yet, we start the engine without a second thought because we have the faith in auto parts we do not see, and we act on that faith. It is the assurance of what we cannot see that allows us to put money in a bank, get married, have a child, make an investment, plant a garden or hire an employee.

A few years ago, our family was seated around a decorated table at my son's wedding reception when my mother-in-law disappeared. One moment she was next to me, and the next she wasn't. She was on the floor! One of the legs on her chair had given way and she had slid silently to the carpet. Fortunately, she was unhurt and laughed at the scene as we helped her up. The restaurant apologized and gave her two free dinners as compensation for her unexpected change of scenery. Yet, when the staff brought her a new chair, she made sure to test its sturdiness before she sat down. Before the collapse, she sat by faith, but now she wants some evidence of her chair's structural integrity.

Each of us demonstrates faith because we trust what is unseen every day. Life would be impossible to manage if we did not. So the question is not, "Do I have faith?" Each of us does. The question that will shape our lives the most is, "Do I have faith in God?"

Responding to God

The definition of faith in Hebrews 11:1 can apply to anything from faith in our babysitter to faith in the safety of an airplane. However, faith in God is more specific. The book of Hebrews tells us that faith in God means to have confidence that God is present even when we cannot see him[3], and trusting that what God tells us is true even before we see it happen.[4] Authentic faith goes far beyond merely agreeing that God exists. Faith in God is a deep trust that prompts us to act on what God says.

> **Faith in God is responding in trust and obedience to God's words.**

Theologian Scot McKnight distills faith down to this: "responding in trust and obedience to God's words."[5] As faith is a response, it means that it is God who acts first. We show faith when we respond obediently to what God tells us. For a human example, imagine a little girl who has never learned to swim standing at the edge of a pool. The father, already standing in the water, calls out, "Jump! I'll catch you!" When she trusts her dad enough to jump into his arms, she is showing faith. She is responding in trust and obedience to his words.

The believers mentioned in Hebrews 11 are examples of faith because they acted in response to God's promise and prompting. They demonstrated and grew their faith by responding to God's word. For example, Abraham showed faith by moving to a country he had never seen simply because God told him to do so. Noah demonstrated faith when he built an ark because God instructed him to do it. Moses responded in trust to God's word when he confronted Pharaoh and demanded he release the Jews from slavery. Each of these men took those risks in response to what they heard God say. Faith is not merely a mystical spiritual feeling or a state of inner conviction; faith is trust expressed through

---

3   Hebrews 11:6

4   Hebrews 11:1

5   Scot McKnight, Galatians; NIV Application Commentary, (Grand Rapids, MI: Zondervan, 1995) p. 121

action. Where does that kind of trust in God come from? Did those believers take those steps because of their faith, or did they have faith because they took those steps? The answer is "both."

The Three-Stage Process

Hebrews 6:12 urges us "… to imitate those who through faith and patience inherit what has been promised." That verse challenges us to do what they did. If we examine the stories of the believers mentioned in Hebrews 11 we see a pattern emerge. Their faith grew as a result of taking three steps:

1) **hear** from God

2) **see** the unseen

3) **risk** taking action.

Hear it, See it, Risk it; that is the process that grows faith. These steps are sequential. The order matters. Step one of the faith-development process is to hear a message from God. Step two is to envision God's message becoming reality. Step three is taking the risk to act on what God says. The result of these three steps is that our faith will grow. All three are essential.

Consider Noah's story. First, Noah heard from God. One day, God told Noah, "I'm going to flood the earth, so build an ark."[6] Noah understands God's message to him. Second, Noah starts to imagine the boat he is going to build. In fact, God helps him visualize the ark he is to build by dictating to Noah the exact dimensions.[7] Noah can see the ark in his mind's eye. Not only does that help him to build it, the image also builds his trust that what he heard from God will happen. Finally, Noah takes the risk of constructing the ark. He risks being mocked by his friends and neighbors for building a huge boat for a flood that no one else thinks will come. What if it doesn't rain? He'll look

---

6   Genesis 6:13-14

7   Genesis 6:15-16

like a fool. What if he can't complete the building job? He will look incompetent. But he takes a step of faith and does it anyway. Noah takes the risk (step three) because he heard from God and he expects that what God said will happen. We can only imagine how Noah felt after the rain started to fall and the water began to cover his neighbors' rooftops. Whatever else he felt, he was filled with greater confidence in God. He had heard what God said and he had acted on it. As a result, his faith was stronger than it was before.

Faith grows as a result of three intentional steps: hear, see and risk.

What if instead of taking these three steps Noah had chosen only to pray and worship? His faith would have been a pale shadow of what it eventually became. If he had never heard God say, "build an ark," he could not have obeyed God. If he had not been able to visualize the ark, he could not have built it. And if he had never gathered the wood and started construction - well, let's just say his family would have been deeply disappointed once the rain started. All three stages were essential. His faith allowed him to take those three steps, and because he took those three steps he grew in his faith. Like Hebrews 6:12 says, we can follow the same process and grow in our faith.

House of Faith

My son Jonathan and his wife Anika pastor an urban campus of our church. Even though they could live more comfortably in the suburbs, they rented a place near the church because they feel committed to living among the people they serve. In recent years, gentrification has caused rents in their neighborhood to rise rapidly. Jonathan and Anika became concerned about being priced out of the area, so they began looking for a house to buy. However, they quickly became discouraged. They did not have a lot of money, and even small houses in bad condition were selling quickly for more than they could afford. They prayed regularly about finding the right house, but month after month their search came up empty.

Then, one day a neighbor told them that the house across the street might become available. Anika had always liked the house, and she asked how to contact the owner. She wanted to make an offer before it went on the open market. Jonathan and Anika made the highest offer they could, knowing it was still well below market value. Initially, the owner was open to negotiating with them but later she said her brother was a co-owner and he wanted to put the house on the open market and maximize their return. Jonathan and Anika were deflated. They knew that meant they would be priced out. They had no choice but to resume their search from scratch. Months went by, and they found nothing. Meanwhile, they were told that the brother had decided to live in the house across the street himself.

Around that time our church held a spiritual growth campaign called "Draw the Circle".[8] Our members were challenged to choose a need in their lives and "circle it" in prayer for six weeks. We hung large sheets of paper on the walls of the worship area and invited people to write their request on the wall, then draw a circle around it. When God answered, they could put a check mark over their circle as a testimony to God's goodness. Jonathan and Anika wrote the word "house" on the wall and circled it. In the following weeks, they prayed for God to give them a house. In particular, Anika prayed for the house across the street. She told Jonathan, "I still feel like that is to be our house." She would look at the house and picture living there.

During this time Anika was meeting with a friend at work once a week for prayer. One day, her prayer partner said, "I believe God is going to make that house yours." Then she named the price she thought they would pay for it. The price she named seemed like a fantasy, though, because it was actually lower than their initial rejected offer. In the meantime, Jonathan and Anika continued their house hunt in vain.

Months later, out of the blue, they received an email from the brother who owned the house across the street. He said that family circumstances had changed and he was not going to move

---

8   Based on the Mark Batterson book by the same name.

to the area after all. He asked, "Are you still interested in buying the house?" Jonathan and Anika immediately responded "Yes!" He replied, "Since you have been so patient, I'll sell it to you for less than you offered before." He named the exact price Anika's friend had predicted months before! They agreed and were given keys to the house so they could work on it even before the sale was completed. For the next couple of months, they scraped off old paint and prepared for future renovations. They knew that it was a risk to work on a house they did not yet own, but they persisted.

The closing took place at the church. After signing the final paper, Jonathan invited the former owner into the sanctuary and showed her the papers hanging on the wall. He pointed to the circle that said, "House." It had a check mark over it. He told the woman about their journey of prayer and trust. Jonathan and Anika's faith went to a new level as a result of hearing, envisioning and risking.

Trust the Evidence

The Hebrews 11 three-stage process grows our faith because it gives us a chance to develop a history with God. That is vital because our trust in God grows in the same way that our trust in people grows: through experience. Trust cannot be demanded; it must be earned. The reason you trust the people you do is that they have repeatedly shown themselves to be trustworthy. When you see that your friends guard your secrets as if they were bank-card passwords, you become confident that you can trust them with even more confidential information. When your employer consistently pays you every two weeks, you grow to trust the company's solvency. Trust is built through repeated positive experiences. That is why there is no one in the world I trust more than my wife Linda. Over several decades of marriage, experience has shown me that I can trust her with the deepest parts of who I am.

We can also grow to trust God deeply through repeated experiences of his faithfulness. When we "hear it, see it and risk it," that creates a track record with God that builds our faith in him. After repeatedly seeing him act in our lives, our trust grows stronger and our doubts grow weaker. There still may be times we cannot understand what is happening in our lives, but having repeatedly experienced God's faithfulness we are able to trust even when we do not have answers.

Don't Wait for a Miracle

It can be tempting to think, "If I could just see a miracle then I'd have rock-solid faith." However, the evidence proves otherwise. If miracles produced great faith, then those who saw Jesus give sight to the blind and make the lame walk would have been his most devoted disciples. But they were not. They all left him before he was crucified. In fact, he was nailed to the cross just days after people saw Jesus raise Lazarus from the dead.

Miracles are wonderful expressions of God's loving power, but they are not an easy shortcut to faith for those blessed enough to see one. The Scriptures show that miracles may boost faith, but they do not create it. When Jesus exhorted us to "Have faith in God,"[9] he wasn't saying, "Go look for a miracle." In fact, when Thomas said he believed because he had seen Jesus risen from the dead, Jesus replied, "... blessed are those who have not seen and yet have believed."[10] Jesus made it clear that he does not expect our faith to be based on miracles.

Hebrews 11 urges us to greater faith by reminding us of the role of faith in the lives of famous Old Testament figures. It is worth noting that miracles are not prominent in the passage[11]. The miracles that do happen in the lives of those we read about occur as they risk taking steps of faith. The writer reminds us of the examples of Abraham, Noah, and others so that we would take the three action steps that they did. Whether or not a miracle occurs, our faith and trust in God will grow.

One might assume that we need a strong faith in order to hear, see and risk. Actually, the reverse is true. We develop a

---

9   Mark 11:22

10   John 20:29

11   Verse 29 refers to the Hebrews crossing of the Red Sea and verse 30 refers to the walls of Jericho falling. However, these miracles are not cited as the source of people's faith; they are the result of the people's obedience that sprang from the faith already present in them.

strong faith as a result of taking those three steps. Each time we hear, expect and risk, our faith grows deeper. Then we can hear, expect and risk responding to God to a greater degree the next time.

If you are not ready to build an ark in your backyard or to put your life on the line for the sake of the Gospel, don't feel inadequate. Just engage the process. Look for an opportunity to hear from God. Then, see in your mind's eye what it will look like when what he promises comes to pass. Finally, take the risk of acting on what God said. The result is that your faith will grow. Let's take a closer look at how to take each of those three steps.

Chapter One Discussion Questions
How Faith Grows

1. Jesus said, "According to your faith be it done to you." In what ways has faith shaped your life so far?

2. The author states, "Everyone has faith." Would you agree? Why or not?

3. Dr. Scot McKnight defines faith as "responding in trust and obedience to God's words." How does this definition evidence itself in the lives of individuals listed in Hebrews 11?

4. Share an experience in which you responded with trust to God's word to you.

5. Faith grows as we "Hear it, See it, Risk it." List them in order from most to least natural for you.

CHAPTER TWO
Hear it

... faith comes from hearing ...

Romans 10:17

OK, I'll admit it; I got choked up. I was watching a video montage of the moment profoundly deaf people heard sound for the first time in their lives. I couldn't keep my eyes from leaking.

The patients had each been fitted with cochlear implants - a device that allowed them to hear voices and sounds they had never heard before. One young woman on the video represented the reactions of the majority of the patients. First, the technician advised her, "It might be a bit overwhelming at first..." Then she activated the device. The woman's face instantly lit up with intense joy and laughter. Then seconds later she covered her mouth and broke into tears, completely overcome. Her life had dramatically changed at that moment. That scene was repeated over and over as one deaf person after another was overwhelmed by the gift of hearing. Strong deaf men who were not used to crying in front of others could not hold back their tears after hearing a human voice for the first time. A mother could not stop laughing after finally hearing her young son's voice. A toddler's face lit up with wonder after hearing his mother speak to him. Each of these people had learned how to get along in life without hearing. But thanks to the implant, a new and richer life opened up for them. They could hear music. They could hear the words, "I love you." Now that they could hear, their lives would no longer be the same.

It is hard for those of us with hearing to imagine what it must be like to go from a life without sound to one filled with voices, noises and melodies. Being able to hear would impact everything from the way we talk to others to the way we experience nature and enjoy movies. The ability to hear would open up the world to us in thousands of new ways.

Opening Spiritual Ears

The ability to hear the voice of God is even more life-changing than receiving a cochlear implant. It changes the way we experience this world and the next. That is because hearing God is the beginning of faith. As we saw in Chapter One, faith is "responding in trust and obedience to God's words." In order to respond to God's words, we first need to hear them.

Each of the stories of faith found in Hebrews 11 starts with people hearing from God and then acting on what he says. Noah was living an unremarkable life with his family when he heard God speak to him. Hebrews 11:7 says, "By faith Noah, *when warned* about things not yet seen, in holy fear built an ark to save his family." Noah heard God's warning of the coming flood, and he responded by doing what God instructed him to do. Similarly, Abraham was minding his own business living in what is modern-day Iraq. Then he heard from God. Hebrews 11:8 says, "By faith Abraham, *when called* to go to a place he would later receive as his inheritance, obeyed and went ...."

God spoke to Abraham and said, "I want you to move to a new land. Just pack and get started, and I'll tell you where you are going when you get there." So, Abraham responded by packing up his household and hitting the road toward Canaan. That response is called "faith." Hearing God was the beginning of Abraham's faith, and it changed his life. Hearing from God not only changed the trajectory of their lives, it also changed history.

It is the nature of God to speak to his people. You cannot read beyond the third verse of the Bible without encountering the words, "And God said ..." God continued to speak from then on. The Bible is filled with stories of people responding to God's word to them. Without the Lord speaking to people, there is no biblical story.

Israel's history would have been completely different if the prophet Samuel never heard the Lord say, "Anoint David as king ..."[12] Without hearing from God, no prophet could have said, "The word of the Lord came to me." At Jesus' baptism, God spoke so that others could overhear him saying, "You are my Son, whom I love."[13] The apostle Paul changed from a persecutor to a planter of the Church when he heard the risen Jesus ask, "Why do you persecute me?"[14] God cleared the way for non-Jews to become part of the Church when he spoke to the apostle Peter and commanded, "Get up, Peter. Kill and eat."[15] At the end of the book of Revelation, the Lord speaks.[16] From the first chapter through the last chapter of the Bible, God speaks. And he has not stopped communicating with his people.

Although hearing from God is the beginning of faith, too many Christians believe they are destined to be spiritually deaf. They acknowledge that God spoke to people in biblical times, and maybe he still speaks to some mystics and super spiritual types today. Still, they assume that "normal" people today do not hear from God. So, they learn to get along with spiritual silence. If the stories of the Bible seem remote and applicable only to people of another era, maybe it is because they involve hearing from God, and we are not convinced we can do that.

However, if you are a Christ-follower, then you have heard from God. Romans 10:17 says, "Consequently, faith comes from hearing the message." If you are a follower of Jesus, somewhere along the way you heard the message of the gospel. When you responded to that, you became a disciple.

How did that happen for you? For me, it was when I was in high school. The guitar player in a Christian band sat down with

---

12 1 Samuel 16:1ff

13 Mark 1:11

14 Acts 9:4

15 Acts 10:13

16 Revelation 22:12-20

me one night at a youth fellowship gathering. He explained to me that Jesus died on the cross for my sins and rose again so I could have a new life. I did not fully understand the message of the gospel that day, but I realized at that moment I could say "Yes" to God in some way. And I did. I responded by praying to ask Christ to forgive and lead me. Faith started to grow in me from then on. If I had never heard that message, I couldn't have started the journey.

A. N. Wilson is a British writer and biographer. Growing up in England, he considered himself a Christian. Years later, he began to wonder if the Easter story was true. By age thirty he had rejected all religious belief. He publicly declared that he was no longer a Christian and became an atheist. He became famous for being a harsh, cynical critic of Christianity and any faith in God at all. In 2004 he wrote a book claiming Jesus was a failed messianic prophet.

But on the Saturday before Easter in 2009, he shocked everyone by publishing an article in which he shared his experience of attending Palm Sunday service. He wrote:

> "When I took part in the procession last Sunday and heard the Gospel being chanted, I assented to it with complete simplicity. My own return to faith has surprised no one more than myself."[17]

A.N. Wilson put himself in a place to hear the gospel, and faith returned to him even when he wasn't looking for it. We come to faith by hearing the good news of the gospel and then responding to it. We grow in faith in the same way.

Ways to Hear from God

My wife communicates with me through a variety of means. Of course, she speaks to me through her words. She can also express herself through a look in her eyes, a touch, a sigh, an expression on her face, a bounce in her step, a gesture, a poem, a song, a note, a gift and so on. Over the years, I have learned to

---

17 The Word on the Wind, p. 101; (Monarch Books, Grand Rapids, MI 2011) Alison Morgan

pick up her signals, whether they are clear or subtle.

God speaks to us in a variety of ways, as well. One of the reasons that we may struggle with the idea of hearing from God is that we have a faulty conception of what it is like to hear from God. We assume that when God speaks it smacks of the supernatural: a thunderous audible voice or a supernatural vision. While those things might happen to some people, it is not what most people mean when they say they heard from God. (If those are regular occurrences for you, then you don't need to read the rest of this chapter!) For most of us, we will hear from God in less dramatic, but just as real, ways. Let me share just a few of those with you.

1. Through Scripture

This is the most reliable way to hear from God. Every time you read the Bible, you are hearing from God. Engaging Scripture aligns us with God's will and ways. It is like fuel for our spiritual fire. The more Scripture we take in, the more likely we are to recognize God's voice when he speaks to us.

Sometimes we may read the Bible and the words seem to apply to us in an unusually personal way. Early one morning in the spring of my senior year of college, I went out to the porch of the old duplex I shared with some other guys in order to spend some time with God. Like most college seniors, I was thinking about my future after school. As I prayed, I opened to Psalm 40 and read the first three verses:

> "I waited patiently for the Lord;
>   he turned to me and heard my cry.
> ² He lifted me out of the slimy pit,
>   out of the mud and mire;
> he set my feet on a rock
>   and gave me a firm place to stand.
> ³ He put a new song in my mouth,
>   a hymn of praise to our God.
> Many will see and fear the Lord
>   and put their trust in him."

Those words resonated powerfully deep within my soul as I read them. In an unexplainable way, I knew that God was telling me that those words would describe my life. God was telling me he would work through me. He would give me inner stability. I was going to express his message in new ways, and the result would be that many people would put their faith in Christ. It was the first time I had ever experienced God speaking to me in such a personal way, and it was amazing and thrilling. Decades later, I have those verses beautifully framed and hanging over my desk. God has been fulfilling those words for me over the years, and they are still guiding me today.

Although I read the Bible almost every day, I don't receive that kind of life-defining word from God every time I open it. I couldn't handle that kind of spiritual earthquake every day! I have found that using a simple method for routinely hearing God through the Bible and deciding to act on what he says keeps my relationship with Jesus fresh. The method I use most often is called "SOAP."

Wayne Cordeiro popularized the SOAP method of engaging the Bible in his book *The Divine Mentor*.[18] SOAP is an acrostic which describes a process for encountering God in the Bible. The steps are:

S = Scripture
O = Observation
A = Application
P = Prayer.

Here is how it works: Read a passage of ***Scripture*** and pick out one verse that stands out to you. Write out the verse; that helps us engage it more thoroughly. Then, write a few ***Observations*** about that verse, such as: What is happening? How would you put that verse into your own words? What do you notice? Next, for the ***Application*** step, write down how you will apply what God said by completing the sentence, "I will ..." Finally, ***Pray*** for God to help you do what you've written, along with any other concerns.

This practice allows us to hear from God consistently,

---

18   Wayne Cordeiro, The Divine Mentor, (Ada, MI: Bethany House Publishers, 2008)

which is the first step toward growing in faith. The more we expose ourselves to the Bible, the more we hear from God in other ways, too.

2. Inner Promptings

Paul Becker is the president of Dynamic Church Planting International, a ministry that trains church planters all over the world. For years, he has made it his regular practice to take prayer retreats, during which he invites God to speak to him. Paul says that the message he hears most often from God is, "I love you." In 2009, though, Paul was surprised by what God told him. At that time, DCPI had an ambitious goal of planting one million churches globally. As Paul prayed about this he sensed God say, "Increase the vision to five million churches." Taken aback, Paul prayed and thought more about what that would mean. Yet today, nine years later, DCPI is right on pace to equip leaders to plant five million churches.

We, too, can hear God speak to us inwardly if we learn to listen. Start by asking God to speak and then stay alert. A prompting from God can take the form of a thought that comes to your mind in an unusually clear or vivid way. Or, it may be an idea that is unrelated to anything you have been thinking about. Some of the thoughts running through our minds are actually God speaking to us. For example, perhaps a friend's name or face comes to your mind as you are going about your day. You decide to call her and she tells you, "I'm so glad you called. I'm going through a tough situation right now and hearing your voice really helped." The idea to call was likely a prompt from God.

Of course, not all our thoughts originate from God. Learning to recognize God's voice requires straining out the mental noise and clutter. Discerning inner promptings from God can be quite subjective. How can we be sure that it is God speaking and not our own inner voice? Truthfully, we will not be absolutely certain. However, promptings from God share a few common characteristics.

For one, a prompting from God will never conflict with the

Bible. If your friend tells you that God is telling him to leave his wife and marry his co-worker, you can be sure it is not God's voice that he is hearing. Also, a prompt from God will be consistent with God's purpose and character. A true prompting sounds like something God would say. If you believe you are receiving a prompt that says, "I love you," that is likely from God because it is consistent with what a loving God would say. In addition, God's voice does not contradict what he has told us before. There is a consistency in God's communication.

When it comes to hearing a prompting from God, there are no guarantees. We cannot be one hundred percent certain that we are hearing correctly. However, the more experience we get in discerning God's prompts the more accurate we will become.

God often leads us more than we realize. For example, some of our desires and goals originate from God. A fascinating detail in Abraham's story is that his father Terah may have been called by God to move to Canaan before he was. Genesis 11:31-32 says,

> "Terah took his son Abram, his grandson Lot son of Haran, and his daughter-in-law Sarai, the wife of his son Abram, and together they set out from Ur of the Chaldeans to go to Canaan. But when they came to Haran, they settled there ... and he died in Haran."

Terah intended to go live in Canaan. It is possible that God planted that idea in his mind. Terah was on his way but he got sidetracked and settled in Haran instead. It was left to his son Abraham to fulfill the family's destiny by responding to God's call and moving his family to the promised land.

Do not hesitate to ask God to speak to you inwardly. Learning to discern promptings from God is a process of trial and error, but keep at it and God will guide you.

3. Through a Prophetic Word

Prophecy is simply "listening to God for others." Just as God will give us a prompting that speaks to our lives, sometimes he will give us a prompting that pertains to someone else's life.

Barak is one of the faith heroes listed in Hebrews 11. Prophecy is key to his story. During a time of crisis in Israel, the judge Deborah gives Barak this prophetic word,

"The LORD, the God of Israel, commands you: 'Go, take with you ten thousand men of Naphtali and Zebulun and lead them up to Mount Tabor. I will lead Sisera, the commander of Jabin's army, with his chariots and his troops to the Kishon River and give him into your hands.'"[19]

Barak did as he was told (though somewhat reluctantly) and became a model of faith because he responded to God's word to him.

Hearing from God through a prophetic word can be greatly encouraging and transformational.

A few years ago, one of our church's campuses was out of space. They had been meeting in a small, low-visibility warehouse for several years. During that time the campus had grown, and despite holding three services per weekend they were completely out of space. They needed a new location, but we were not able to find a suitable facility available in the area. Dale, our campus pastor, led the leadership to pray and search, but after two years they came up empty. Finally, we learned of a building for sale just a few miles away. It was larger, more attractive, and in a better location than the one we were leasing. We negotiated with the owner's agent for about six months. Throughout that time members of the campus took turns walking around the building praying for God to give it to us. They were there several times a week at all hours of the day and night. (It's amazing no one called the police!) After long negotiations, the agent finally said she thought we had a deal that would work. Though we were offering less than the asking price, she felt it could be agreeable to the owner. It turns out that it wasn't. We were back at square one. After years of searching and months of praying and circling the building, we had nothing. No prospects. No leads. Meanwhile,

19 Judges 4:6

the campus was stuck and could not grow. Dale was discouraged.

About ten days later, Dale was working at the outgrown space when an Indian man he had never met walked in and introduced himself as the pastor of an Indian congregation in the city. After a brief conversation, the visitor was preparing to leave when he asked Dale if he could pray for him. When Dale said, "Yes," the man asked whether Dale would be open to hearing a word from God. Again, Dale said, "Sure." As the pastor prayed for Dale and the congregation, he said God was telling him that they needed a new building. There was no way for that man to have known that the campus had been searching for one. It had not come up in their earlier conversation. Nonetheless, he went on to say that God had another building for them and started to describe it. He accurately described all the unique features of the building we had just unsuccessfully tried to purchase! Dale was astonished and encouraged. When he was at his lowest, God had sent him a word.

A few months later a congregational leader proposed that we lease part of the facility we had tried to buy. The owner agreed. The price was substantially higher than what we were paying, and Pastor Dale knew they were staking the future of the campus on its future growth. Sure enough, when the congregation moved in they grew substantially. The members continued to circle the building in prayer, asking God to give us the facility. Two and a half years later we purchased the building for nearly the same price that was rejected a few years earlier.

God spoke through a prophetic word and the people responded. They took a risky step, and as a result, they saw God act and their faith grew to a new level.

4. Through Other People's Words

There are times God will speak to us through the words of someone who has no idea that God is using them to communicate with us. That makes it different from a prophetic word.

One spring day of my freshman year in college my girlfriend (now my wife) Linda casually said to me, "Someday you would make a good pastor." She was not trying to give me career counseling. She did not feel like she had a message from God. Still, those words stuck with me. It started me thinking and praying about being a pastor. It seemed right. Several years later I entered seminary and I have spent the rest of my life in local church ministry. (And Linda is still hoping that someday I'll make a good pastor!)

After I had been in ministry for about six years, a fellow pastor said to me, "Steve, you should think about planting a new church." I had never considered that before. Over the months that followed, we talked frequently about what that would look like. His enthusiasm for church planting was infectious. Over time I came to sense God's call to plant, and the result has been Crossroads Church. Now our church is organizing to catalyze 100 new churches. God used the words of someone else to speak to me.

Hebrews 11:20-22 reminds us of how God spoke this way through the patriarchs to their descendants:

> By faith Isaac blessed Jacob and Esau in regard to their future.
> By faith Jacob, when he was dying, blessed each of Joseph's sons, and worshiped as he leaned on the top of his staff.
> By faith Joseph, when his end was near, spoke about the exodus of the Israelites from Egypt and gave instructions concerning the burial of his bones

God's word through another person became an important link in the faith development of those who heard.

These are just some of the ways we can hear from God. Expect him to speak to you. When we hear from God we can respond in faith.

Stay Under God's Faucet

If it seems like it has been a while since you have heard from God, do not despair. Instead, stay under God's faucet. That is, consistently put yourself in a place you can hear God's message. Just like we can't complain our glass is empty when we don't put it under the stream, we can't expect to hear from God if we are not in a position to hear.

Worship regularly where you will hear God's message through song and word. Open the Bible daily. God wants to speak to you. Spend time around other believers. Small groups are an excellent way to do that. Serving teams can also help you rub shoulders with people through whom God will speak to you. Stay around faith-filled people. They are contagious!

God still speaks, and hearing him is the beginning of faith. What might God be saying to you today? What is God saying through this book so far? Take note of it. It doesn't have to be earth-shaking, just specific. In order to obey it, we need to be able to say it. So, don't let any message from him pass you unnoticed. Hearing from God is where faith is born, but in order for our faith to grow we need to do more than hear. We need to expect it to happen.

Chapter Two Discussion Questions
Hear it

1. What was the best news you ever received?

2. What is your first reaction when you hear someone say, "God told me ..."

3. In your opinion, is it possible to grow in faith without hearing from God?

4. How do you most clearly hear from God? Through Scripture, inner promptings, a prophetic word, words of other people or some other way?

5. What would it mean for you to put yourself "under God's faucet" this week?

CHAPTER THREE

See it

"Holy is imagination, the gateway of Reality into our hearts."[20]

— Thomas Kelly

[God] took [Abram] outside and said, "Look up at the sky and count the stars—if indeed you can count them." Then he said to him, "So shall your offspring be." Abram believed the Lord ...

Genesis 15:5-6

Amy Purdy was nineteen years old when, without warning, she lost both of her legs below the knees. One day she was a vibrant and healthy young woman, brimming with dreams of adventure and a passion for snowboarding. The next day she felt like she was coming down with the flu. Less than 24 hours later she was lying in the hospital in a coma. She had contracted bacterial meningitis. Doctors gave her a two percent chance of survival.

Amy recovered, but when she woke up she had lost her spleen, her kidneys, the hearing in her left ear and both legs below the knees. She was left physically and emotionally broken. In the months that followed, Amy battled depression and struggled to learn how to walk on prosthetic legs. On a deeper level, she searched for how to live out an unexpected life.

---

20   Thomas R. Kelly, A Testament of Devotion (New York: Harper, 1941), 33.

Amy's turning point toward wholeness came when she began to daydream about what she wanted her future to look like. She imagined herself walking gracefully, helping other people and snowboarding again. "I didn't just see myself carving down a mountain of powder," she said. "I could actually feel it. I could feel the wind against my face and the beat of my racing heart as if it were happening in that very moment. And that is when a new chapter in my life began." Four months later, Amy got back on a snowboard. At first it was painful and frustrating. Her knees and ankles would not do what she wanted them to do. Once, she created a sensation on the slopes when she fell during a run and her new legs – still attached to her snowboard – went flying down the mountain without her.

Still, Amy persisted. Finally, the day came when she was able to live out her vision of snowboarding with the wind in her face. She later went on to win back-to-back World Cup gold medals, making her the highest-ranked adaptive female snowboarder in the world.[21]

Imagination was the key that unlocked Amy's new life. And imagination is vital to growing our faith.

Seeing the Unseen

Imagination is not mere fantasy or make-believe. Though it sometimes gets a bad rap, the capacity to imagine is given to us by God. It is what allows us to share in God's creative nature. Imagination allows us to prepare for future reality. World-class athletes prepare to compete by visualizing themselves performing at the highest level. In their minds' eye, they see every movement of a flawless performance before they execute it. They harness the power of imagination to achieve their very concrete goals.

We use our imagination more than we realize. When we truly expect something to happen, we can picture it happening before it occurs. For example, after we buy concert tickets, we can imagine

---

21 Amy Purdy, Ted Talk https://www.ted.com/talks/amy_purdy_living_beyond_limits

what it will be like to be in the arena, shoulder to shoulder with the crowd. We see the band on stage. In the words of Hebrews 11, we have the assurance of the concert we do not yet see. After we make reservations for a vacation at the beach, we say we are looking forward to the trip. Even our language indicates that we see the as-yet-unseen. In our mind's eye, we can picture ourselves relaxing on the sun-drenched beach or diving into crashing waves. When we look at our tickets, we have confidence of the vacation we hope for. We enjoy thinking about the experience because anticipation extends and amplifies the fun of a vacation.

Anticipation is also an exercise in faith. When we visualize what we have not yet seen with our eyes, we are using faith muscles. People of faith use their imaginations to link God's promises with future reality. Faith grows when we respond to what God says by seeing it in our mind's eye before it becomes a reality. In his classic book, *With Christ in the School of Prayer,* Andrew Murray says,

> Faith is very far from being a mere conviction of the truth of God's Word or a conclusion drawn from certain premises. It is the ear which has heard God say what He will do **and the eye which has seen Him doing it.**"[22]

Murray described faith as hearing from God and seeing in our mind's eye God fulfilling his word before it ever happens. Seeing the unseen is the second step of the faith development process, and the Bible contains many examples of believers doing exactly that.

Imagination in Hebrews 11

The faith heroes of Hebrews 11 first envisioned God's promises before they acted on them. In fact, God even helped many of them picture what he was going to do so that they could better respond in faith.

For example, God asked Noah to prepare for a flood even though Noah had never seen one before. Hebrews 11:7 says, "By faith Noah, when warned about things not yet seen, in holy fear

---

22 *With Christ in the School of Prayer*, p. 96 Whitaker House, 1981

built an ark." As we saw in the first chapter, after God told Noah to build a boat, he gave Noah a detailed description of what the boat should look like. That made it possible for Noah to form the mental image he needed to take the step of faith of building the ark.

Hebrews 11 reminds us that God also fueled Abraham's faith by giving him a mental image of stars to help him picture his promised descendants before any of them were born.

> "And by faith even Sarah, who was past childbearing age, was enabled to bear children because she considered him faithful who had made the promise. And so from this one man, and he as good as dead, came descendants as numerous as the stars in the sky."
>
> - Hebrews 11:11-12

God promised Abraham, "Your descendants are going to become a great nation."[23] That would be startling news for any guy to hear when he is seventy-five years old and doesn't have any kids. It is not surprising that Abraham needed some help believing that would happen. Initially bewildered by the Lord's promise, he responded by saying, "But Lord, I don't have any children, and my servant is going to inherit everything of mine."

God knew that Abraham's faith needed some help, so he gave Abraham an image:

> He took him outside and said, "Look up at the sky and count the stars—if indeed you can count them.' Then he said to him, 'So shall your offspring be." Abram believed the Lord.[24]

God prompted Abraham to use his imagination to help his faith grow. He pointed him to an image that he could turn to again and again. From then on, every night when Abraham stood outside his tent and looked up at the sky, he could imagine his descendants as numerous as the stars he saw. God gave Abraham a mental picture of what the promise would look like when fulfilled.

Imagining the fulfillment of God's word was an important step in building faith in Noah and Abraham. It is important for

---

23 Genesis 12:2

24 Genesis 15:5-6

building our faith, too. Faith involves seeing the unseen, and the faculty we use to do that is our imagination. Hearing from God is vital, but it is not enough to make our faith soar. We also need to pay attention to what we are seeing in our mind's eye. Jump-starting our faith might be as simple as picturing what it will look like when God's word becomes a reality in our lives. When you read the Bible and come across a promise that resonates in you, take a moment to imagine it as fulfilled. What would it look like if that promise was to become real in your life? What would you feel like? What would be happening, and what details of your life would be different?

Seeing the Promise Honors God

It is not presumptuous of us to imagine God's work before it happens. Rather than offending him, it honors God because it means we trust his character and his word to us.

While getting ready to move a couple of years ago, my wife Linda came across one of her old college notebooks. She saw that on the last page she had written the words, "Mrs. Stephen Cordle" half a dozen times. There was nothing else on the page - just line after line of the phrase, "Mrs. Stephen Cordle." When she saw that page, she let out an embarrassed laugh. She remembered writing that when we were still students in college. We were engaged, but at that time her name was still Miss Linda Keck. She was trying out her future name by writing in her notebook. She was envisioning herself as my wife. That did not strike me as presumptuous. In fact, I found that rather endearing–even flattering. I was glad Linda was confident that I would follow through on my promise to marry her. If during our engagement she had instead told friends, "I'm going to wait to see if we get married. I'll believe it when it happens," I would have felt hurt, not honored.

Which response to God's word honors him more, to hedge in doubt or to anticipate that what God says will happen? It is not arrogant to picture what you are praying for. That is what faith does. When you trust the one who gave you the promise, then you can picture it happening. God responds to that trust.

One day Jesus was teaching in a house when the roof came off. It turns out that a determined group of men had not been able to get past the crowds to see Jesus, so they climbed on the roof and made a hole in order to lower their paralyzed friend down into the room for a chance to be healed.[25] Matthew 9:2 says, "When Jesus saw their faith, he said to the man, 'Take heart, son; your sins are forgiven.'" When Jesus "saw their faith," what exactly did he see? He saw their level of expectancy. You don't go to the trouble of pulling a paralyzed guy onto a roof if you aren't convinced something is going to happen. Jesus was not offended by their presumption; he was moved by their faith.

See Something, Say Something

Our level of expectancy can be fragile. It can fade in the face of delay or pain. To increase it, say what you see. Our words carry power to shape our thinking and attitudes. If you want your faith to grow, pay attention to what you are saying.

Matthew 9 contains two more incidents of healing. In both, Jesus' power is released after people speak about what they expect Jesus to do. First, a synagogue official says to Jesus, "My daughter has just died, but come and lay your hand on her and she will live."[26] That distraught father verbally expressed to Jesus what he pictured happening: she will live. And she did. Then, a woman who had a chronic, 12-year bleeding condition told herself, "If I just touch his garment, I will be healed." She did not feel worthy to address Jesus directly, but she spoke to herself expressing what she expected. She could see in her mind's eye her hand reaching out and touching Jesus' cloak and her body becoming whole again. That is exactly what happened.

Even Jesus used the power of speech to build faith. When he arrived to raise the official's dead daughter, he declared what was going to happen before it did. "She is not dead, but sleeping," he told others. When people laughed at this, Jesus sent them out of the area because they were not adding faith to the situation with

---

25 Matthew 9:1-8

26 Matthew 9:18-26

their expressions of ridicule.

It is not our words that make miracles happen. Jesus said to the bleeding woman, "Your faith has healed you." Her faith, though, was strengthened and expressed through her words. What we see in our imagination builds faith. What we say helps us to see what God intends. It is not always easy or natural to maintain a clear mental picture of what it will look like when God's word is fulfilled. When we read a scriptural promise that we sense God wants to apply to us, it is easier to agree with it and then forget it. If we want our faith to grow, it is worth the effort to envision what God says becoming reality.

Praying in Faith

Understanding that faith involves seeing the unseen will influence the way we pray. There have been times I have prayed about a problem, only to feel worse afterward. The reason for that is that I was praying the problem instead of praying the answer in faith. By "praying the problem," I mean spending time describing and dwelling on my struggle. When we pray in faith we pray the solution, not the problem. For example, if your teenage son is sick, praying the problem may sound something like this:

> "Oh Lord, Lucas has mono ... he's so sick. He has no energy at all. He probably won't be able to get to school at all this week. If he doesn't get better soon he won't be able to finish his classes this semester and he might lose his eligibility for soccer this year, and he loves soccer. Lord, it's going to crush him not to be able to play. He's going to be so depressed. Please help. Amen."

Praying like that rehearses the problem, as if God does not know about it. God does not need us to describe all the potential disasters that could spring from the situation. Doing so builds fear rather than faith, and it will leave us more depressed than when we started.

In contrast, praying in faith means seeing the answer to your prayer and praying that. You pray,

> "Oh Lord, Lucas has mono ... he's so sick. He has no energy at all.

But you have the power to heal him! You have said to ask, seek and knock and you will answer. Lord, right now I ask you to drive out that mono from his body – give him the energy to get back to class, to play soccer and to do all the things you made him to do. Heal him; help him know you touched his body. Help him grow closer to you through this experience. Thank you in advance for this."

When we pray in faith we do not ignore or deny the existence of the problem. We recognize the need and then visualize the answer as we pray. In this case, we see our son full of health and energy. That is a prayer of faith.

The Old Testament story of Hannah demonstrates how seeing the unseen changes prayer from a painful experience to an uplifting one. Hannah was childless, and it caused her great pain. One day she went to the tabernacle to beg God for a child. She was so filled with grief that she cried aloud to God. The priest Eli heard her and reprimanded her because he thought she was drunk. She explained,

> "Do not take your servant for a wicked woman; I have been praying here out of my great anguish and grief." Eli answered, "Go in peace, and may the God of Israel grant you what you have asked of him." She said, "May your servant find favor in your eyes." Then she went her way and ate something, and her face was no longer downcast.[27]

Hannah was sobbing in prayer until Eli told her that her prayer would be answered. Once she envisioned her prayer as answered she became optimistic and hopeful. She could imagine the answer to her prayer, and her faith grew.

One of the reasons that specific prayers carry more power than general ones is that we can visualize the answer to a specific prayer. General prayers are so vague that we cannot tell whether they have been answered, and thus we cannot exercise faith through imagining that answer.

If you have been praying about a problem, what would it

---

27 1 Samuel 1:16-18

mean to imagine the answer to your prayer? Might it mean seeing your bills as paid in full and something is still left in your bank account? Or, it could be seeing yourself as free from that destructive habit. Imagine yourself waking up in the morning embracing Jesus' love and victory, not defeated and recycling the same tired script. Does God have the power to do that? Does he want that for you? The answer is yes. So expect that enough to imagine it. The Bible says that when you confess your sins to God that you are totally forgiven, clean in His sight.[28] Can you see yourself that way? Or do you continue to look in the mirror and see yourself as a stained, guilty failure? Choose by faith to see future reality by forming a mental picture of what God says.

The Limits of Visualization

Now let me be clear that visualization does not create reality. God does. Our mental picture of the future is merely an action step that helps us build trust that what God says will happen. Faith puts us in a position to experience what God will do.

Some Christians get concerned about references to visualization because they have heard it associated with secular and New Age spiritualists who teach, "Picture it and it will become a reality"[29] or "Your thoughts will create your future." For example, one book with which I am familiar claims that sustained positive thinking will attract wealth and health or whatever else we might want.[30] We are right to shun that kind of self-centered teaching. Ironically, those teachers correctly recognize that there is power in visualization. However, their approach does not lead to a kingdom mindset, because authentic faith starts with what God says, not with what I want. Remember, faith is a response to God's word and promise to us. Visualization is an important step in responding to what God says, but it comes after we hear from God. It is the second stage of faith that flows out of first hearing from God. It does not come out of a selfish desire on my part.

---

28 1 John 1:9

29 Neville Goddard, *Law of Attraction Success Stories*

30 Rhonda Byrne, *The Secret*

Christians need not reject the biblical practice of envisioning God's promises becoming reality simply because visualization has also been pressed into the service of other belief systems. After all, so have worship, fasting and other biblical practices. The difference lies in the source of the object to be visualized - is it God, or ourselves?

Any time we pray about the future we will imagine something, vividly or not. A vital faith imagines God's word becoming reality. Of course, our imaginations are limited and fallible. Our pictures of the unseen will not always be accurate. Plus, God can and will surprise us. Ephesians 3:20 says, "Now to him who is able to do immeasurably more than all we ask or imagine, according to his power that is at work within us ..." Even our imperfect images will strengthen our faith when focused on God's purposes. God gives us the capacity to imagine because we need it in order to keep following him for the long haul.

Imagination Counters Delay

We might assume that if God makes a promise that it will be fulfilled quickly and without problems. A reading of Hebrews 11 tells us that is not so. Most of the men and women of faith highlighted in Hebrews 11 encountered obstacles and delays after they heard God speak.

Abraham was 75 when God told him his descendants would become a great nation. He had to wait another 25 years until his son was born. That's a long wait! There had to have been times he doubted it would happen at all. His wife had given up and told him to have a child with one of the servants. She even laughed when a messenger from God told her she'd finally have a child within the year.[31] Through those long, childless years Abraham could look up to the stars and remember what God told him. He had a mental picture of his promised future. If we can visualize the fulfillment of God's word to us, we will be able to endure the wait during the times it appears that nothing is happening.

---

31 Genesis 18:12

Each time I drive along the main highway that borders our church's original location, my eyes are drawn to glance up to our facility. Twenty years ago I passed by that location and saw nothing but scrub trees and a sign that read, "Future home of Crossroads Church." For months, every time I drove by that tree-covered hill, I would look up and think, "Someday there is going to be a building right there, and it's going to house a life-giving church." I'd imagine a building rising from the spot. I could see it in my mind. However, that dream was not becoming reality. Our congregation was 150 people meeting in a rented restaurant banquet room. We did not even have the money to clear the property, let alone to hire a general contractor. That meant we could not obtain construction financing. We were stuck.

During the months nothing was happening, seeing the unseen helped sustain me. I was convinced that God wanted our church to be built on that spot, so I pictured it rising there. Each time I drove by, I'd imagine a roof-line poking up out of the trees and the parking lot surrounding the building. I would pray, "Lord, this is your mission - make that building a reality!" I didn't realize it at the time, but I was engaging the second phase of faith building.

Waiting periods seem to be part of the faith journey. When God's word is slow to become reality, you need an inner picture to draw on. When you have prayed and nothing seems to be happening, start visualizing the answer. When you are tired of waiting, imagine God's future.

Some of the heroes of faith in Hebrews 11 never got what God promised fulfilled in this life. They had to wait for eternity. However, Hebrews 11:13 says that they saw it anyway: "They did not receive the things promised; they only saw them and welcomed them from a distance." Seeing the answer from a distance helped those believers go the distance in faith.

Imagination Withstands Trials and Fear

Have you ever heard from God and then things got worse instead of better? Moses did. He confronted Pharaoh and demanded, "Let my people go." Pharaoh responded by making the Hebrew slaves' life even more miserable. When they finally escaped they became stuck between the Egyptian army and the Red Sea. Just because we hear the promise of God does not mean that life will become simple and easy. When everything seems to go from bad to worse, we can resist fear by refocusing on the picture of God's word becoming reality.

Late in Abraham's life God repeated the word picture he had given him years earlier. This time, however, God adds another image for emphasis: "I will surely bless you and make your descendants as numerous as the stars in the sky and as the sand on the seashore."[32] God added the phrase "sand on the seashore" to his earlier image of stars in the sky. I like to think that God did this not only for emphasis but also for those stormy days when Abraham could not look up and see the stars overhead. At those moments, he could look down and envision his descendants. He could look forward to the fulfillment of God's promise every day, whether it was sunny or rainy.

If you find that worry and anxiety are coming more easily to you than faith and confidence in God's promises, take control of your imagination. Focus on what God says and picture what it will look like when it happens. Create that visual in the theater of your mind. Seeing the unseen builds a confident assurance that what God said will happen. Imagination alone does not accomplish God's purposes. God's word coupled with imagination prepares us to take the next step that will build faith, as we will see in the next chapter.

---

32 Genesis 22:17

Chapter Three Discussion Questions
See it

1. Would you call yourself more of a "dreamer" or a "realist"? How does that show up in your life?

2. Why is hearing from God not enough to grow our faith? How might our faith be weakened if we do not expect God's word to become reality?

3. What is the difference between hoping God's word happens and expecting it to happen?

4. What is the difference between arrogant presumption and faithful expectation?

5. What keeps you from more fully expecting God's word to come to pass?

6. Is there something you are expecting from God right now? Can you describe it?

CHAPTER FOUR

Risk it

*"Faith is taking the first step even when you don't
see the whole staircase."*

— Martin Luther King, Jr.

"A pastor should not know how to do this," I thought, as
I stood in a hole up to my waist. I was gripping a survey pole
while a bulldozer operator peered through an instrument in
order to confirm the elevation of the catch basin he was creating.
The absurdity of the moment struck me. I knew nothing about
construction, but here I was, overseeing a major building project
that relied almost exclusively on volunteers. If it didn't work, we
would be in big trouble. Or, at least, I would be in big trouble.

Our church was just a few years old and worshiping in a
rented restaurant banquet room. We were growing slowly but
steadily, but we needed a building of our own. I knew that if we
did not take that step soon we would lose momentum, and our
long-term future would be threatened. We ran a capital campaign
and raised more money than was reasonable for a church our
size. Still, it was not enough to hire a general contractor for the
project. That meant we could not obtain a construction loan.
Sensible voices told us to wait to build until we could raise more
money. However, in my mind, delaying a few more years was
not an option. I believed God's vision for us required a building
sooner, not later.

As our leadership discussed the situation, one member
approached me privately and said, "Let's build it ourselves."
Building with volunteer labor seemed like a crazy idea at first,
but the man who proposed it worked in the construction indus-

try, so we did not immediately write it off. The more we studied the possibility, the more we began to imagine how it could work. Sure, it was risky, but if we could do it, we would get into our own building within a year at half the normal cost. We decided to go for it.

The project was a huge undertaking. Not only did we need to construct the new building, we also had to carve a parking lot out of an adjoining hillside, extend the public sewer line up a state road, negotiate right-of-ways, obtain permits and build a new public street that included a cul-de-sac. Due to the scope of the project, we also needed to recruit additional volunteers from beyond our church. And oh yes, we had to find a source that would provide us 80 percent of our building supplies on unsecured credit, too. Our denomination promised to give us a mortgage once we had an occupancy permit, but if we started the project and could not finish it, we would be left in serious debt with no means to repay. That would almost certainly mean the death of our young church — and maybe my future in ministry.

Nonetheless, after months of preparation, we put the ceremonial shovel in the ground one Saturday morning in March. For the next nine months, volunteers from our church (and from other churches in the region) sacrificed vacations, nights and weekends acting as a construction crew. Finally, on the first Sunday of November, we celebrated the opening service in our beautiful new facility. There was just $1,000 left in our church's bank account and some leftover bills that we needed to address, but we had done it. Soon after that, the church began to grow rapidly; and best of all, our faith was stronger, too. The risk paid off.

Faith is Risk

John Wimber once said that faith is spelled R-I-S-K. There is no such thing as a "sure-fire" step of faith. If we want to grow in faith, we need to get used to taking steps that feel risky, because faith traffics in the unseen. As 2 Corinthians 5:7 says, "we live by faith, not by sight." There are no guarantees when it comes to acting on faith.

Faith requires action. We may hear from God and even envision that word becoming reality, but until we take action on what God says we are only dreaming. The book of James says, "... faith by itself, if it is not accompanied by action, is dead."[33] In fact, hearing from God without acting on what God says will weaken our faith, not build it.

Again, faith is a positive response to God's words. So, it is no surprise that Hebrews 11 illustrates the faith of the heroes of the Old Testament by describing their actions:

"By faith Abel brought ..."
"By faith Isaac blessed ..."
"By faith Joseph ... spoke ..."
"By faith Moses ... chose ..."

Hebrews 11:33-34 also refers to the faith of other unnamed saints using verbs:

[others] through faith conquered kingdoms, **administered** justice, and gained what was promised; who **shut the mouths** of lions, **quenched** the fury of the flames, and **escaped** the edge of the sword.

Abraham is a great example of faith because he took risks in order to respond to God. He packed up his household and headed for a land he had never seen before. That was a risk. What if his clan was attacked by bandits and never made it to Canaan? What if the land was not as good as their land in Haran? God had spoken, so Abraham took the risk and went.

Abraham's biggest risk of faith came after he thought his future was secured. After decades of waiting, he and Sarah had a son. Abraham saw that God made a way to fulfill the promise that he would have many descendants. Then, God spoke again. This time God asked Abraham to do the unthinkable. God told Abraham to sacrifice his son, Isaac. Abraham did not want to imagine

---

33 James 2:17

that word becoming real. As a father, how could he bring himself to do such a thing? How could he kill the only means by which God's promise could be fulfilled?

Yet, Abraham's faith propelled him to respond with action. He took Isaac up the mountain. He gathered wood for the sacrifice. He placed Isaac on the altar. At the last instant, as Abraham was about to do what God asked, God stopped him. Abraham had demonstrated that his faith and trust were so strong that he would do whatever God asked, even if it made no sense to him.

While we will not be asked to do what Abraham did, each follower of Jesus will face moments when the thought of acting on God's word makes us highly uncomfortable. Jenn and her husband, Jon, had one of those moments during a six-week prayer initiative at our church. They sensed God prompting them to take a major risk. Jenn was praying for her brother and his wife because they had been unable to conceive a baby after three and a half years of trying. She was also praying for her brother to put his faith in Christ. Then, she read in her devotional book that if we want God to answer bold prayers, sometimes we need to make bold moves.

As she prayed, she started to feel strongly that she was supposed to give her bother and his wife a crib as a gift. "But that was craziness," she said to herself. She told her husband what she was feeling prompted to do, and he agreed that it was crazy, risky and potentially hurtful to the couple. They told their small group about the idea, who agreed that it was crazy, but BOLD. After a week, Jenn and her husband agreed that they couldn't shake the feeling that they were supposed to send them the crib. So, with great reluctance they did. Jenn was petrified and prayed earnestly that this wasn't the biggest mistake of her life. She loves her brother and would never want to hurt him with a gift that seemed to mock his deepest unfulfilled desire. The day came for the delivery to be made, and her brother received the gift with silence (which is uncharacteristic for him). His wife was moved and renewed in her own faith. Success!

Jenn was pleased and breathed easier. However, the biggest

success was yet to come. She and Jon, along with their small group, kept praying and fasting. At one meeting they even chanted, "fill the crib." Finally, God said, "Yes." Jenn wrote,

> After three-and-a-half years my brother and his wife are now expecting a baby (maybe more than one!). And I am expecting my brother to return to Christ. He and his wife will attend church this Easter Sunday, and I am overwhelmed by joy and the magnitude of what Christ can do when we pray boldly, expectantly and are obedient to God's pull on our hearts.

Jenn and Jon could have played it safe and simply prayed private prayers. Instead, they took the risk to act on what they believed God told them to do. As a result, their faith grew, her brother's family's faith was reignited, and their small group is bolder in their trust in God.

Courage to Act

Taking a step of faith sounds exciting when everything works out well in the end. But what if it doesn't? What if we act on what we believe God is telling us and everything seems to fall apart? What if it turns out to be nothing like we imagined?

That's what happened to the Apostle Peter. In Matthew 14, we read that he took one of the most famous faith steps in history, and things didn't go exactly as he expected.

The disciples had struggled to get across the lake all night, and they weren't making much progress (and most of these guys were professional fishermen!). The waves were battering them and the wind was howling. It was pitch dark - about 3 a.m. They must have been exhausted and cold. As they struggled, they were stunned to see Jesus coming toward them, walking on the water.

> When the disciples saw him walking on the lake, they were terrified. "It's a ghost," they said, and cried out in fear. But Jesus immediately said to them: "Take courage! It is I. Don't be afraid." "Lord, if it's you," Peter replied, "tell me to come to you on the water." "Come," he said. Then Peter got down out of the boat, walked on the water and came toward Jesus. But when he saw the wind, he was afraid and, beginning to sink, cried out, "Lord,

save me!" Immediately Jesus reached out his hand and caught him. "You of little faith," he said, "why did you doubt?"

Matthew 14:26-31

Peter had followed the faith-building process. He heard Jesus' word to him ("Come"). He had a clear image of what it would look like to walk on water because he was watching Jesus do so. He pictured himself out there walking with him. Peter even took a step out of the boat into the dark and onto the deep, churning water that was being driven by gale force winds. That more than qualifies as a risk. Then, after taking some steps ... he sank.

Isn't that what we fear about a step of faith? What if it doesn't turn out like we hope it does? What if we go under? That is the fear that kept the other disciples in the boat.

Steps of faith require courage. Jesus told the disciples they needed courage.

When the disciples saw him walking on the lake, they were terrified. "It's a ghost," they said, and cried out in fear. But Jesus immediately said to them: "Take courage! It is I. Don't be afraid."

Matthew 14:26-27

Peter did as Jesus said and took courage. The other disciples didn't. That is not to say that Peter did not feel fear. He was in the same boat as they were. The difference was that Peter didn't let his fear control him. As Michael Hyatt said, "Courage is not the absence of fear. Courage is the willingness to act in spite of my fear."[34] Courage is feeling anxious and doing it anyway. Every step of faith requires that kind of courage.

On October 14, 2012, Felix Baumgartner set the world record for the highest skydive when he jumped from a helium balloon [34] miles above the earth. On his freefall he reached a speed of over 800 miles per hour, becoming the first person to break the sound barrier without a vehicle. This feat was not as simple as fall-ing out of a door and opening a chute. If Felix did not maintain

34 https://michaelhyatt.com/courage-is-not-the-absence-of-fear/

perfect form, he would go into an uncontrollable spiral and be ripped apart in mid-air. During Felix's descent there were a few tense seconds of wobbling, but to everyone's relief he managed to regain control and landed safely.

I cannot imagine what it was like for Felix to be suspended in the earth's stratosphere and then open the door, step out onto a ledge and look down. At that moment Felix knew that if he jumped, he would either make history or he would die. Yet, knowing that, he stepped off the ledge. It was a literal step of faith.

Today, Felix Baumgartner is famous for making sky diving history. What many do not know is that Felix almost didn't make that jump because he was terrified ... of enclosed spaces. The cockpit of the balloon that carried him into the stratosphere was very small. Felix had such a severe case of claustrophobia that at one point in the training he actually resigned from the mission. He had to go through intensive therapy in order to be able to climb into that tiny delivery vehicle. Here was a guy who had the courage to stand 24 miles above the earth, step into the emptiness and risk getting ripped apart on his descent, but he was terrified of sitting in the capsule. Everyone feels fear at some point.

If we want to grow in our faith, there will be moments we need to act on God's word despite our discomfort. I wish that fear went away after a few experiences with taking steps of faith, but it doesn't. I have taken many steps of faith in my forty years of following Jesus, and I still feel anxious when it is time to take another significant one.

Where can we find the courage to risk it and grow in our faith? Peter's story can give us clues.

First, *focus* on God's word to you.

The key moment in Peter's adventure of walking on the water was when he heard Jesus tell him to step out of the boat. Until then, Peter was just a spectator.

> "Lord, if it's you," Peter replied, "tell me to come to you on the water." "Come," he said.
>
> Matthew 14:28-29

Peter would not step out of the boat until he heard Jesus tell him to do so.

Peter was smart enough to know that there was a big difference between having an interesting idea and hearing from Jesus. Once Peter heard Jesus' word, that was all he needed. If Jesus told Peter to come, Jesus would be responsible for the outcome. The reason Abraham could head up the mountain with Isaac was that he left the results in God's hands. If God told him to do it, God would take care of the future.

The same principle holds true for us. Our minds will come up with lots of reasons why we should not take a step of faith in obedience to God's word to us. They usually begin with, "What if ..." The only way to combat those scenarios is to fill our minds with what God said.

For example, when we read in the Bible that God calls us to give generously, we might balk. "What if I give and then I can't pay my bills? What if my savings is not enough?" To combat that fear, we remind ourselves of what God told us then leave the results to him. I regularly hear stories of people who gave out of obedience to God, and to their delight found that they had all they needed after all. As a result, their trust in God grew. To build the courage to act, remind yourself of what God said, and then you will be able to take that step of faith.

Second, to get the courage to risk it, choose to *give up control*. The instant Peter stepped out of the boat he was no longer in control. He was walking on the churning water with nothing but Jesus' power to hold him up. He is above water only because Jesus is keeping him there.

If we demand to be in control of everything that happens in our lives, we will find it difficult to risk faith. If we knew how little control we actually have over our lives, we would find it a little easier to release the illusion and trust God enough to take the risk of obedience.

Years ago, I was asleep in bed when my phone rang at around 2 a.m. A member of our church was dying, and would I please come to the hospital? "Of course," I replied and started to get dressed. My wife woke up enough to hear the conversation. As I was about to leave the room, she rolled over in bed and said, "Take the van." The van was her vehicle. I drove a little Honda Civic because it got great gas mileage. I never drove the van unless the whole family was in it. Still, I said, "OK, I will." There was no traffic in the middle of the night. As I neared the hospital, I stopped for a red light at a four-way intersection. When the light turned green, I pulled the van ahead just in time to see a blur out of the corner of my eye, followed by an explosive, jarring crash. A drunk driver going the wrong way down a one-way street had slammed into me. Stunned, it took me a moment to realize that the front end of my van was destroyed. I traveled the rest of the way to the hospital courtesy of an ambulance and made my pastoral visit after a quick stop in the Emergency Room. It turns out that my neck and back were sore, but otherwise I was unhurt.

Looking at the totaled van the next day, I realized that if I had been in my Honda Civic, it was highly likely that I would have been killed. Why was I still alive? It wasn't my brilliant planning or driving skill that kept me safe. It was because Linda had turned over and said, "Take the van" on the spur of the moment. (That was the only time before or since that she did something like that.) On a deeper level, I believe God had spared my life even when I didn't know I was in danger. I love to feel in control of my life, but the longer I live the more I realize how little of it I have. It is God who is in control. Taking a step of faith reminds us of that fact in a vivid way.

A third key to finding the courage to risk a step of faith is to **be willing to fail.** Peter's experience on the water could not be called an unqualified success.

> But when he saw the wind, he was afraid and, beginning to sink, cried out, "Lord, save me!" Immediately Jesus reached out his hand and caught him. "You of little faith," he said, "why did you doubt?"
>
> Matthew 14:30-31

In the end, Peter failed ... or did he? True, Peter's faith did not hold. He took his eyes off of Jesus and became intimidated by the threatening waves. You can almost hear him thinking as he stepped toward Jesus, "Wait! What am I doing?! I can't walk on water!" Yes, Peter started to sink. Then again, for a few incredible moments, Peter also *walked on water!* He alone stepped out of the boat and became the only person not named Jesus to walk on water. The other disciples didn't sink, but they didn't walk on water, either.

The first time I went skiing, I proudly announced at the end of the day that I did not fall once. The experienced skiers I was with were unimpressed. They said the point of my first day is not to avoid falling; the point is to enjoy skiing. They said that if I didn't fall, I was being too cautious. I needed to take more chances in order to learn. Kids don't mind trying things they aren't good at; they are accustomed to learning by trial and error. Adults, on the other hand, generally don't like to fail at anything. After all, we don't want to look foolish. The fear of failure causes us to limit what we attempt. However, the purpose of life is not to avoid failure, it is to follow Jesus' call. Sometimes, we will fail as we learn.

We will not always get it right when we risk steps of faith. Sometimes we will misunderstand God's word to us. We may act at the wrong time. We don't need to fear that. Yet, when Peter went down, Jesus didn't let him drown. If we mess up while taking a step of faith, Jesus will be there to pick us up, just like he was for Peter. When you are prompted to share your faith, don't shrink back for fear you might do it wrong. Don't decline a job opportunity that God sends to you just because you aren't sure you can do it perfectly. Don't be afraid to fail – Jesus will catch you.

Finally, in order to get the courage to act, *just do it*. Like John Ortberg says, "If you want to walk on water, you've got to get out of the boat." In the film *We Bought a Zoo,* the character played by Matt Damon famously says, "Sometimes all you need is twenty seconds of insane courage. Just literally twenty seconds of embarrassing bravery. And I promise you, something great will come of it." There's a lot of truth in that. It didn't take long for Peter to get out of the boat. Twenty seconds might be all it takes for you to dial that phone number and make that call, or to open your mouth and say, "Let me tell you about my experience with Jesus", or to say "Yes" to the Spirit's prompt to yield your life to Christ. When we are acting on God's word to us, something great will come of it, whether we see it or not.

Risk, in and of itself, does not cause our faith to grow. It is risk in response to hearing and seeing God's word that results in a deeper faith and trust in Him. When we take a step of obedience in the face of uncertainty, God is honored and his power is released. We become aware of our dependence on the Holy Spirit and of our need to intentionally rely on God. The resulting experience creates a track record with God that is personal and life-changing.

It is said that at the end of people's lives it is not the things they have done that they regret most; it is what they did not do that haunts them. When you hear from God, no matter how big or small the issue may be, risk taking that step of faith. Step into the life God has prepared for you.

Chapter Four Discussion Questions
Risk it

1. What is the riskiest thing you have ever done? How would you describe your risk tolerance?

2. Why is our faith hindered if we both hear and see God's word but do not act on it? (James 1:22).

3. Pick an individual listed in Hebrews 11. What risk did they take?

4. What are you doing now that if God doesn't act you are in trouble?

5. Is there a step of faith you are avoiding because it is too risky?

Part Two

Defending our Faith

CHAPTER FIVE

Troubleshooting

I decided to take up golf about fifteen years ago. Until then, I hadn't been interested in the sport; but I got tired of responding, "I don't play," when asked to go on an outing. So, when a friend of mine offered to set me up with some quality clubs, I accepted. He is a terrific golfer and he patiently offered me pointers. In spite of his help, I quickly discovered why the game has been called "a nice walk ruined." For every good shot I hit, I hacked a couple of lousy ones. I realized that if I was going to enjoy the game, I needed to get better at it. My wife noticed my frustration and gave me some golf lessons as a birthday gift.

My instructor showed me that a golf swing has three parts: backswing, impact position, and follow-through. A breakdown in any one of those three parts will result in the ball flying (or rolling) toward an unintended landing spot. A textbook back swing might look impressive, but if my head moves or my weight lags back at the impact position, I will be unhappy with the result. Even if I execute a flawless follow through, if the take away on my back swing is offline, my score will suffer. In order to hit the ball well, I need to execute all three parts of my swing properly.

Unfortunately, a few lessons were not enough to fix my swing. It was going to take a lot more practice and patience than I was willing to invest in order to become a better player. One afternoon, after spraying the ball around the course, I decided that I no longer needed to pay money to be frustrated. So, I put my clubs in the corner of the garage where they sat for ten years until my wife put them out on the curb with a sign reading, "Free." In the heat of frustration, it was easy to write off my golf game by saying, "I'm not a good golfer." It would have been more accurate for me to say, "My wrist position at impact is inconsistent." If I had been motivated enough to take the time to work on that technique, I could have improved.

Like a golf swing, our faith also has essentially three components: hearing from God, seeing its fulfillment in our mind's eye and risking an action step. Just as a flaw in any stage of the golf swing leads to predictable trajectory problems, a breakdown in any one of the three stages of faith results in a weakened faith. However, we don't need to react to our faith problems as I did to my golf frustrations. Instead of generalizing, "I'm not good at faith," we can take targeted corrective steps.

In the next few chapters, we will trouble-shoot three of the most common problems we encounter as we seek to live by faith. These are: doubt, fear and sin. It is hard to respond to God's word with a confident trust when we are wracked with doubt or fear. Sin creates a barrier between us and God, introducing uncertainty and distance into our relationship with him. In order to grow in faith, we need to know how to counter these oppositional forces.

Doubt, fear and sin each can be traced to a breakdown in one of the three components of faith. Specifically:

- Doubt arises from a loss of hearing from God.
- Fear is a failure of imagination – that is, imagining disaster instead of envisioning God's word coming to pass.
- Sin is a step in the wrong direction instead of risking a step of faith.

When these predictable forces strike, we do not have to surrender to them by concluding, "I'm just a fearful person," or, "I'm just the doubting type." God can empower us to resist the temptation to put our faith out on the curb or stop investing in our relationship with him. We can overcome those faith killers by addressing their underlying causes. Each of the next few chapters will focus on how to heal a mindset or habit that undermines our faith.

At its core, faith is relational. It is not an entity unto itself.

Faith is responding in trust to the voice of the one who created us. We do not have faith in a principle; we have faith in a person. Our faith is a cooperative partnership with God. Faith is initiated by God's word to us, but Jesus also indicates that we have a part to play ("Have faith"). A dynamic personal relationship with God cannot be reduced to a set of mechanistic rules. So, the following chapters' insights are not to be understood as a formula for creating faith. Rather, they are practical handles on doing our part in receiving life-giving faith. Addressing obstacles like doubt, fear and sin is like removing obstacles that stunt the growth of a garden. Pulling weeds, fertilizing and irrigating the ground do not cause plants to grow, but they create the environment that allows them to do so.

Similarly, God causes our faith to grow, but we have a role in making our hearts receptive. Learning to neutralize these common faith enemies can give us a solid base from which to grow. Or, to use a different analogy, eliminating these faith problems is like working with a marriage counselor. In order to strengthen their relationship a couple may be coached in certain issues like communicating respect or eliminating thoughtless actions. By deliberately working to minimize hurtful attitudes and habits, they clear the way for love and trust to thrive.

We can expect the overcoming of faith barriers to require sustained practice. If practice is essential for perfecting a golf swing, how much more so for replacing unhealthy spiritual habits with healthy ones? We live in an age of "instant." If a website page takes more than a second to download, we mutter and move on to another. We have been programmed to expect quick changes in everything from stoplights to weight loss.

Overcoming faith-killers does not usually happen quickly. Doubt, fear and sin are generally the fruit of assumptions, experiences and mindsets that have been established over years or decades. So, it will take some time and intentional application of God's truth to see lasting change in our trust level. Do not be discouraged. Press in. Those mindsets and identity issues will be reshaped because you have the Holy Spirit at work in you.

CHAPTER SIX

Doubt
Spiritual Hearing Loss

*"It is not as a child that I believe and confess Jesus Christ.
My hosanna is born of a furnace of doubt."*

— Fyodor Dostoyevski

Take a guess, what do these people have in common: C.S. Lewis, Pope Francis, Martin Luther, Ann Lamont, Charles Spurgeon, John Calvin, Mother Teresa? Answer: they are all great Christian thinkers, and they all wrestled with doubt.

Sadly, doubt is an unmentionable subject in many Christian circles. Believers who readily discuss their salaries or sex lives feel ashamed to admit that they wrestle with doubt. They hope it doesn't show and that they will be able to kick it before anyone finds out. Doubt can feel disorienting, distressing or even threatening. After all, isn't doubt the exact opposite of what defines us as Christians – that is, to have faith? Won't doubt disqualify us from membership on the Jesus-followers team? We might wonder if it is a signal that our faith is about to crumble completely. Doubt leads to a sense of isolation when we assume that we're the only one dealing with it.

The truth is, most of us will wrestle with doubt at some point. The Barna Research group found that two out of every three Christians will experience spiritual doubt, questioning what they believe about God or their religion.[35] Pope Francis spoke about his own experience with doubt during a 2013 General Audience in St. Peter's Square. He said, "Who among us has not experienced insecurity, loss and even doubts about their journey of faith?

---

35 https://www.barna.com/research/two-thirds-christians-face-doubt/

Everyone! We've all experienced this, me too. Everyone." So if you have doubt, take heart, you are not alone! Even Abraham, Gideon and other heroes of faith mentioned in Hebrews 11 went through seasons of doubt.

Perhaps overcompensating for this unwarranted shame associated with doubt, numerous recent books and sermons assert that doubt is a positive experience because it causes us to dig deeper into our relationship with God. There is an element of truth to this; Barna's research shows that almost all evangelicals say their time of doubt improved their faith.

But to be accurate, it is not doubt that strengthens our faith; it is the resolving of doubt that produces spiritual strength. Those who have made it to the other side of doubt with a firmer, bolder faith can look back on that spiritually unsettling season and recognize that it left them more confident in the end. Remaining in a state of doubt, however, does not help us. Even though doubt is not generally spiritually fatal, we need to be honest about it: doubt is not a virtue to which we are called to aspire. The Bible never refers to doubt in positive terms. Jesus never exhorts his followers to doubt more. When Peter tried to walk on water and started to sink, Jesus asked him, "You of little faith, why did you doubt?" (Matthew 14:31). Doubt is never heralded as the gateway to the abundant life in God. Nowhere do the Scriptures say that the key to answered prayer is doubt. To the contrary, James 1:6 says, "But when you ask, you must believe and not doubt." We are not saved through doubt but through faith. Have you ever said to yourself, "If only I had doubted God more, my life would have been so much richer?" If you look back over the last five years of your life, could you say, "If I had only doubted God more, I would have experienced much more peace, love and joy?" I doubt it.

Most of us doubt at some point. When we do, we should not feel afraid, ashamed or alone in it. That doesn't mean we need to resign ourselves to live with it either. The risen Jesus did not shame or reject his disciple Thomas for doubting his resurrection. Yet, when he appeared to Thomas he said, "Put your finger here; see my hands. Reach out your hand and put it into my side. Stop doubting and believe" (John 20:27).

Stop doubting and believe. Sounds simple. How do we do that?

If we are going to deal constructively with doubt, we need to know what it is and what it is not.

Alister McGrath writes that doubt is not skepticism[36] – which is to adopt "Prove it" as a default response to any claim to truth. The favorite phrase of the skeptic is, "Yeah, right." Thomas was more of a skeptic than a doubter when he said, "Unless I see the nail marks in his hands and put my finger where the nails were, and put my hand into his side, I will not believe" (John 20:25). Thomas was open to seeing evidence for the resurrection, but lacking it, he could not believe.

Doubt is not unbelief[37] – which is the decision not to believe. While skepticism admits, "I cannot believe," unbelief declares, "I will not believe." Unbelief will not seriously seek or consider evidence for faith. The decision has been made; faith is no longer an option. Richard Dawkins, a prominent figure in the "New Atheism" movement, exemplifies the decisive nature of unbelief. He wrote,

> "The God of the Old Testament is arguably the most unpleasant character in all fiction: jealous and proud of it; a petty, unjust, unforgiving control-freak; a vindictive, bloodthirsty ethnic cleanser; a misogynistic, homophobic, racist, infanticidal, genocidal, filicidal, pestilential, megalomaniacal, sadomasochistic, capriciously malevolent bully."

Dawkins made up his mind not to believe, and he made sure everybody knew it.

So, if doubt is neither skepticism nor unbelief, what is it? Doubt is a question. While unbelief declares certainty, and skepticism demands proof, doubt has questions. They may surface when we have an experience that doesn't make sense to us, or when we confront an idea that does not fit with our previous understanding. For example, if our expectant prayer goes unanswered, we might wonder, "Is God listening to me?" or "Does God really care about me?" Or, if we see a news report about children

---

36 McGrath, Alister. Doubting. Downers Grove, IL: IVP Publishing, 2006 p. 13

37 ibid. p. 13

being massacred for political reasons, we might begin to question God's goodness. "How could a loving God allow innocent children to be murdered like that?"

Abraham and Sarah had seasons of questioning doubt. God promised them a son, but many years went by and still, they were childless and elderly. Then, three angelic visitors told them that they would have a son by the following year. Sarah heard the promise but could not imagine it being fulfilled. It seemed crazy. Sarah literally laughed when she heard the promise; "After I am worn out and my lord is old, will I now have this pleasure?" (Genesis 18:12). Her question revealed she doubted the visitors' message.

Gideon is another faith hero mentioned in Hebrews 11. He, too, expressed doubt. When the Midianites were overrunning Israel and stealing the nation's food, God called Gideon to lead an army to drive them out. When the angel of the LORD appeared to Gideon, he said,

> "The LORD is with you, mighty warrior."
> "Pardon me, my lord," Gideon replied, "but if the LORD is with us, why has all this happened to us? Where are all his wonders that our ancestors told us about when they said, 'Did not the LORD bring us up out of Egypt?'"
>
> Judges 6:12-13

Gideon heard that God was with Israel, but he questioned that because he saw their enemies overrunning the country. What he saw around him didn't line up with what he was hearing from God, and so he doubted God's word to him.

Doubt and Faith Co-Exist

An atheist group in England made headlines around the world by posting ads on London buses which read, "There's probably no God. Now stop worrying and enjoy your life." Christian groups responded with their own ads, reading: "There definitely is a God. So join the Christian party and enjoy your life", and "There IS a God. Believe. Don't worry and enjoy your life." My hunch is that many riders secretly agreed with both groups' ads, depending on the day. Faith and doubt are not polar opposites; it is people who believe, who doubt. Those who don't believe are certain in their unbelief. They do not have questions. We can only doubt what we already believe. So, there is often a mixture of faith and doubt in us.

Matthew 28:17 is one of the more remarkable verses in the New Testament. It describes the moment Jesus' eleven closest disciples gathered on a mountain in Galilee shortly after Jesus rose from the dead. Just days before, their hearts and hopes had been shredded when Jesus was tortured and killed. Then, some of the women of their group amazed them with the news that the tomb was empty, and that an angel had told them that Jesus had risen from the dead. On the mountain, the resurrected Jesus appeared to them. Matthew 28:17 says, "When they saw him, they worshiped him; but some doubted." Let that sink in. They both worshiped and doubted. The risen Jesus is standing in front of his disciples in his resurrected body, completely whole. It was such an awe-inducing sight that most spontaneously worshiped him, "... but some doubted." How can they be looking at the resurrected Jesus and yet doubt? If you have followed Jesus for any length of time, it probably doesn't surprise you. Doubt is often co-mingled with faith.

In Mark 9, a father brought his demon-possessed boy to Jesus. The disciples had tried to heal him but they couldn't. So, the father turned to Jesus and pleaded, "... if you can do anything, take pity on us and help us." "If you can?" repeated Jesus. "Everything is possible for him who believes." Immediately the boy's father exclaimed, "I do believe; help me overcome my unbelief!" (Mark 9:22-24).

At some level, the father surely believed in Jesus' power or he would not have brought his son to him. Still, we can understand why he might have had questions. For years he had seen his son suffer; those images were very vivid in his memory. He had asked the disciples for help and they couldn't help. He heard stories of Jesus making the blind see and the lame walk. He believed Jesus could heal. The question was, would he? Would he heal his son as he had others? He believed, but he also doubted.

If you have doubt, it is likely you also have faith. Faith is not "all or nothing." We can have faith and still wrestle with nagging questions.

What Causes Doubt

Most doubts start and are fed by an inability to hear from God.

As we saw in chapter one, faith is responding in trust and obedience to God's words. If we do not hear God's words, we cannot respond with trust and obedience. When we lose the habit of "hear and obey," doubt grows in the vacated space in our soul.

Doubt has both an intellectual side and a personal side. Hebrews 11:6 tells us, "And without faith it is impossible to please God, because anyone who comes to him must believe that he exists and that he rewards those who earnestly seek him."

This verse lays out two requirements for faith, and hearing from God jump-starts both.

First, we must "believe he exists." There is an intellectual component to faith. We can't respond in trust to a God we don't believe exists. As I will discuss below, if we are questioning the existence of God, it is very helpful to become familiar with the work of great thinkers who deal with the subject. We will find that it may not be possible to "prove" the existence of God, but faith is not irrational.

Even while we seek to understand the rational basis for belief in God, there is nothing like personally hearing from God to settle the matter. It is hard to deny the reality of someone who is speaking to you. When Abraham, Noah and Moses each heard God give them instructions, their question was not whether God existed; their question became whether to obey. Hearing from God helps us settle the issue of God's existence.

Secondly, Hebrews 11 tells us that we must "believe he rewards those who earnestly seek him." There is a relational aspect to faith. We do not respond in a trusting way to someone we do not know. We can believe God exists yet not believe God will get involved in our lives. We might believe that God created the universe and guides the broad arc of human history, while not believing that Almighty God will intervene in our lives. Faith believes that God rewards those who seek him.

If we do not hear from God, he will seem distant. It is only when we hear God's promises that we can trust and respond to them. Noah would not have built an ark unless he had heard God tell him to do so. Abraham would not have prepared to sacrifice · Isaac unless he had heard God's promise. "He who had embraced the promises was about to sacrifice his one and only son" (Hebrews 11:17).

To respond to God's promises with trust and obedience, it is vital to believe God does what he says he will do. That starts with hearing the word of God.

Curing Hearing Loss

In a sense, this entire book is about how to reduce our doubt and grow our faith. To do that, we need to hear God's word, see it and risk it. When doubt starts to cloud our spiritual vision, even that process can seem too much to handle. To get back on the path, the first step is to return to where we began: with a word from God. To overcome doubt, we must renew our focus on hearing from God. Remember, Romans 10:17 "Faith comes by hearing ..." It all starts there. When we find ourselves questioning the presence or goodness of God, hearing from God brings reassurance.

Imagine a ninth-grader seated on a bench in front of the school waiting for his mother to come to pick him up. As time ticks by, he sees other parents arrive and his classmates pile into their family cars and head to their homes. But there is no sign of his mother. His mind begins to churn. Is she on her way? Did she forget she needed to pick him up? What if she had an accident? Soon he is the only student left waiting for a ride. He thinks back to when he left the house that morning. He thought he remembered her saying she was going to pick him up, but now he isn't sure. Finally, he pulls out his cell phone and calls her. When she answers she reassures him that, yes, she is on her way and will be there in ten minutes. Satisfied, he pulls out his headphones and sits back to enjoy some music while he waits. He had started to question whether his mother was coming for him, but after he heard her voice promising she was on her way, the doubt evaporated.

When we start to doubt God's reality or involvement in our lives, hearing his word brings us back onto firm ground. When we are not sure God is there, hearing his voice settles the issue. When we question whether God's promise can be trusted, it is reassuring to hear him repeat it. Without regularly hearing from God, our faith will grow dormant and weaker, opening us up to doubt. That's because it disrupts the chain reaction that builds our faith: to hear it, see it and risk it. We can't envision what we have not heard, and we cannot risk acting on what God says if we don't know what that is.

It is easy to get distracted and preoccupied with voices other than God's. There are literally thousands of messages coming at us every day. At the flick of a switch, we can hear the voices of cable news pundits, Taylor Swift's opinions and the claims of advertisers. We can't completely shut off ourselves from all competing voices, but it is vital that we prioritize hearing from God. It will feed our faith and starve our doubts.

When you are struggling with doubt, the top priority is to do whatever it takes to hear from God. Accept no excuses; eliminate all barriers that keep you from hearing from God.

As chapter two states, the most reliable way to hear from God is to read the Bible. It is not the only way to hear from God, but it is an essential one. We need daily interaction with the Bible in order for our faith to stay strong and growing. Reading the Bible will not cause all our doubts to vanish, but engaging what God says to us in the Bible is the first step toward faith. It will kick-start the three-stage process of hearing it, seeing it and risking it. God's word to us is the fuel for our faith's fire. The more God's word is present in our hearts, the higher the flame of faith will rise in us.

In the remainder of this chapter, I'd like to offer a number of "hearing aids" that can help you hear the message from God that you need during a time of spiritual questioning.

Listen for God about what matters. Doubt is a question, but not every question is of equal importance. Some matter more than others. "How many angels can dance on the head of a pin?" is the epitome of a meaningless question. Medieval churchmen may have hotly debated the question, but we know that our trust in God does not depend on the answer. On the other hand, "Did Jesus rise from the dead?" is a vital question. The Apostle Paul says that the answer determines the reality of our faith.

Some people stumble needlessly because they see debatable, secondary issues as essential to the faith. One scientifically minded agnostic I know cannot say "Yes" to the Gospel because he cannot accept that the world was created in six days. Even though I tell him that we can follow Jesus no matter what we believe about that issue, he sees it as inseparable from the Gospel. Yet, in 1 Corinthians the Apostle Paul dealt with a number of disputable topics that were causing controversy among the believers in Corinth. Toward the end of the book, he reminds them that not every matter of doctrine is of equal importance. He writes: "For what I received I passed on to you as of first importance: that Christ died for our sins according to the Scriptures, that he was buried, that **he was raised** on the third day according to the Scriptures (1 Corinthians 15:3-4). Whether we believe in the resurrection matters more than whether or not we eat meat.

Our questioning can actually be an indicator that our faith is maturing. One way we grow is by releasing a superficial understanding of faith and embracing one that has more foundation. A superficial, unexamined faith won't stand up against exposure to new ideas and people. College students who believe only because "that's the way I was raised" find their faith in a very vulnerable position after they arrive at college. They will be confronted with questions they had never considered and don't know how to answer. They need a faith that stands up under exposure to other cultures and ideas.

I recall talking with a young man who was struggling with the reliability of the Bible. He had been raised in a Christian home where the authority of the Bible was presumed and never questioned. As a college student, though, he had been confronted with information and issues he had never considered before, and it caused him to question all he had assumed. He heard about writings like the Gospel of Thomas and the Gospel of Judas, and he wondered if ancient church leaders had conspired to keep dissenting ideas on the sideline. So, he questioned the validity of his faith.

I told him that just because a manuscript was ancient and bore the title "Gospel" did not make it authoritative. There were many books about God circulating during that time, just like there are today. They were not all of equal reliability. The Church examined all the documents and affirmed the books that were consistent with the truth as taught by Jesus to those who knew him on earth. Those became the New Testament.

The student assumed because humans were involved in the writing and recognizing of the Scripture, that made the Bible suspect. What he learned was that it is not a Christian concept to deny that humans play a role in God's activity. It is non-orthodox groups who insist on revelation without human involvement. For example, the LDS Church (Mormons) say that founder Joseph Smith received the Book of Mormon on golden plates directly from an angel. Muslims say that Mohammed received the Koran dictated by God. Underlying this is the assumption that human involvement sullies the work of God. But Christians declare that God not only works through humans, God became a human!

That young man pursued the answer to his question and gained a new appreciation of an important Christian truth: that God works through people to accomplish his purpose. Realizing this allows me to see God at work in my small group even when it seems ordinary or messy. It helps me understand God might even work through me.

Confusing central questions with secondary ones will give more power to doubt. Listen for what matters.

Listen for God about your next step. When Gideon doubted God's call to lead the fight against the Midianites, he asked why Israel was being invaded if God was with them. He did not get an answer to his question. Instead, "The LORD turned to him and said, 'Go in the strength you have and save Israel out of Midian's hand'" (Judges 6:14). God told Gideon to act, then his doubt would be resolved.

Often, the resolving of our doubt is one action step away. Listen to God to discern that step. When you read the Bible, look for how to apply what you just read. If you doubt whether the Bible is true, read it and act just on the parts you do believe. Don't try to resolve every question at once. Act on what God says, and you will start to experience him in ways that will build your faith. You will expose your heart to Jesus' ways and your trust will grow. As Martin Luther King once said, "If you can't fly, then run. If you can't run, then walk. If you can't walk, then crawl, but whatever you do, you have to keep moving forward."

If you can't muster the faith to take a huge step, take a small step, then another one, and another one after that.

Listen for God through a mature believer. When you are doubting, confide in another mature follower of Jesus. Faith is contagious, and connecting with people of faith will help yours.

Chapter ten will explore this more fully. For now, let me encourage you not deal with doubt in isolation. If you are wrestling with doubt, be sure to get into community with some other followers of Jesus. Make it a point to worship with others, but also build relationships with other believers. Get involved in a small group or another environment where you can know people and be known. Connect with people who won't gasp in shock that you ask a question, yet who are settled enough in their own faith to be helpful.

Listen for God through scholars. Enduring faith can handle key questions with intellectual integrity. The good news is that no matter what question you have, you are not the first person in history to ask it. Brilliant, faithful followers before you have explored the issue and can give you the benefit of their insight. It is worth the effort to look for answers because they are out there. Christianity is not irrational.

There are outstanding books available that address questions about God, the problem of pain and the uniqueness of Jesus, among other topics. For starters, you might try:

- *Reason for God* by Tim Keller,
- *The Case for Faith* by Lee Strobel and
- *The Problem of Pain* by C.S. Lewis.

We don't need to have all the answers, but to beat doubt we need the answers to two questions: 1) Is God there? 2) Is God good? These questions impact our faith because our answers to them will determine how we will respond to what he says to us.

We cannot fully answer every question, but that is fine because not all questions keep us from growing in trust and obedience to God. Relating to the infinite eternal God will produce some mystery. Having no questions might not be a sign of a firm faith. It could indicate we've reduced our vision to what we can manage and understand.

Listen to the Spirit's conviction. Doubt is not a sin, but sin can feed doubt (see chapter eight). That is because sin creates a barrier of guilt between ourselves and God. We start to feel distant from God when we are consciously doing what he says not to because the only way to keep disobeying him is to ignore him. When we are sinning and out of step with God, the Holy Spirit will prompt us to change. Listen to him.

All of the above factors are not relevant during every season of doubt. If you are in a period of spiritual questioning, look over this list and consider which one or two of these may be most important to address. However, be sure to prioritize hearing from God. Without hearing from him, our faith grows weak.

I went to college about eighteen months after becoming a follower of Christ. I vividly remember wrestling with doubts like, is God really there? Did Jesus really rise from the dead? Is the Bible reliable? I read a lot of books that defended the faith and talked about these questions with many people I respected.

Today, I rarely wrestle with doubt about the big stuff - God's existence and goodness. I can't pinpoint the moment doubt about God's reality and power receded, but I believe there are two reasons it no longer attacks in a sustained way.

First, I do not doubt less often because I have more answers, but because I have more evidence. I have accumulated years of experiences with amazing answers to prayer, unexplainable "coincidences," and so many moments of experiencing the whisper of his voice that turn out to be true. Taken alone, any one of those is not enough to persuade a skeptic, but together they form an experience of faith and a relationship with God that has become part of the fabric of my being.

Secondly, I am comfortable with some unanswered questions. I have found that faith is not having all the answers, but having enough confidence in a few essential truths to trust God with my life. There are some mysteries about God that I realize no one will ever understand this side of heaven, and that is OK. For now, I am content to respond the best way I know how to the word of God as I hear it.

Chapters Five and Six Discussion Questions
Doubt

1. If you could ask God one question now, what would it be?[Q2]

2. The author states,"God causes our faith to grow, but we have a role in making our hearts receptive." Would you agree or disagree? Does that thought encourage or discourage you?

3. If doubt is a question, how might you explain the doubt of those seeing the risen Jesus (Matthew 28:17)?

4. What questions does Gideon have (see Judges 6)? How are they resolved? What role does hearing from God play?

5. Which of the following means of hearing God have been most helpful in resolving your doubts? Which might be most helpful for you now?

- Listen for what matters

- Listen for your next step

- Listen to a mature believer

- Listen to faith-filled scholars

- Listen to the Spirit's conviction.

Q2 https://www.whatchristianswanttoknow.com/small-group-ice-breakers-25-good-questions/

CHAPTER SEVEN

Fear
A Failure of Imagination

Though fear may come, faith will overcome.

—K. Sutter[38]

Fear is a choice. So is faith

—Craig Groeschel

"What have I gotten myself into?" I wondered silently. I was on a 15-hour flight to Mozambique with our associate pastor. We were on an exploratory mission for our church. Although my colleague had served as a missionary to Mozambique, I had never been there and I knew nothing about the country. So, on the long plane ride over, I started reading the travel guidebook I had brought along. It said that the country was recovering from civil war and was the fourth poorest country in the world at that time. I learned about the many scenic and beautiful parts of Mozambique. I read about their culture and history.

Then, the book's section on travel safety stated that carjackings were known to occur on the nation's main highway, so it was important not to be on that road after dark. As I began to think about the possibility of experiencing random violence in a foreign country, I grew increasingly uneasy. Maybe this trip wasn't a good idea after all.

---

38 C. Anderson, K. Sutter, Faith to Move Mountains, (Independently Published, 2017). 10

I decided to close the guidebook and read my Bible instead. I happened to open to Acts 18 and read about Paul's ministry in the town of Corinth. I came to verses 9 and 10, which read:

"One night the Lord spoke to Paul in a vision: 'Do not be afraid; keep on speaking, do not be silent. For I am with you, and no one is going to attack and harm you, because I have many people in this city.'"

Acts 18:9-10

Those verses resonated in my soul in an unusually personal way. I sensed that through those words, God was reassuring me about our trip. He was telling me, "Do not be afraid ... no one is going to attack and harm you, because I have many people in this city."

After landing, we had a productive and enjoyable week making connections for future ministry. We met fellow believers who were gracious and hospitable. On our final morning we were preparing for a three-and-a-half-hour trip north to visit a school. I thought to myself, "This week has gone well. Now, the worst thing that could happen would be if we made the trip north with no trouble, visited the school and then broke down just after leaving the school. If that happened, we would not be able to get back before dark." I have no idea why I dreamed up this anxiety-producing scenario. We had not had any car trouble the entire week. After an uneventful trip north and a fruitful visit at the school, we got in the car and headed back to the city. You guessed it. About ten minutes into the return trip, the car rolled to a stop. We were broken down on the side of the road. For added fun, there were no buildings in sight except for the one to our immediate left, and its sign read, "Traditional medicine" (what many would call, "witch doctor"). It was a surreal moment. I thought, "You have GOT to be kidding me! How could this be actually happening?!" I was pretty sure that God was involved in this somehow, but I had no idea why or what he was doing.

It turns out the car's radiator cap had gone bad and all the water had boiled out. After some searching, our driver found some water, refilled the radiator and nursed the car down the highway for fifteen to twenty minutes. Then, it all boiled out and we broke down again. We repeated this time-consuming procedure a few more times. By that time, I realized that there was no way we were going to get back to town before dark. In fact, there was a significant possibility that we would not get back to town at all that night. I was stressing out big time. As much as I hate to admit it, I was in the grip of fear.

Faith in Reverse

Maybe you can remember a moment when you were gripped by fear. Each of us faces fear of some kind. It might be the fear of death, failure, or rejection. Some fear spiders, financial lack, getting fat, or heights. Some fear flying.[39] Fears assail us with different levels of intensity and in various forms:

- Worry is dwelling on what might happen if …

- Anxiety can range anywhere from a vague sense of unease to full-blown panic attacks.

- Fear comes from anticipating a threat or actual danger.

Matthew 8 recounts a day Jesus' disciples were gripped by fear when they faced a life-threatening storm at sea.

> "Then [Jesus] got into the boat and his disciples followed him. Suddenly a furious storm came up on the lake, so that the waves swept over the boat. But Jesus was sleeping. The disciples went and woke him, saying, 'Lord, save us! We're going to drown!' He replied, 'You of little faith, why are you so afraid?' Then he got up and rebuked the winds and the waves, and it was completely calm. The men were amazed and asked, 'What kind of man is this? Even the winds and the waves obey him!'"
>
> Matthew 8:23-27

---

39 Someone said, "I'm not afraid of flying, it's the crashing and burning I'm concerned about."

When the disciples started out, they expected to make a routine trip across the Sea of Galilee. A boat ride that should have taken two to three hours at most turned into a fear-inducing, life-and-death struggle. How did the disciples end up in this situation? They were following Jesus! Verses 23 and 24 tell us, "Then he got into the boat and his disciples followed him. Suddenly a furious storm came up on the lake ..." The disciples were following Jesus and a storm hit them anyway.

We may be tempted to think that if we are following Jesus we can expect smooth sailing. We might assume that if we are staying faithful to Jesus that all our doctor check-ups will produce good reports, that our jobs will be secure and that our kids will live happily ever after. However, the disciples followed Jesus into the boat and they ran right into a ferocious storm that no one saw coming. I can imagine someone today suing Jesus for breach of contract. After all, Jesus' job is to protect us and to make us feel safe, right? Well, no. That idea doesn't come from him,[40] and it is not the reality for most Jesus followers. Jesus never promises to prevent bad things from happening to us, but he does empower us to live without fear of those things.

In the midst of the storm, Jesus asks, "You of little faith, why are you so afraid?" The answer to that question might seem obvious. "Look around! Waves are crashing over the boat! We're in a deadly storm!" Jesus' question, though, implies that if the disciples were filled with more faith, they would have less fear.

Jesus repeatedly told his followers, "Do not be afraid." There are at least 365 places in the Bible that God says some variation of the message, "Do not fear." That's one for every day of the year! There is a reason the Lord is so emphatic that we not fear. It is not simply that God does not want us to feel bad or uncomfortable.

It goes much deeper than that. God tells us not to fear because fear prevents us from living by faith. Faith is responding to God's words, but fear keeps us from doing that. When fear attacks us, it

---

40 In fact, Jesus told us the exact opposite. He promised: "In this world you will have trouble. But take heart! I have overcome the world." - John 16:33

takes control. It drives us. We have a border collie named Molly who is afraid of loud noises. Thunder, fireworks or gunshots, even in the distance, will drive her under our bed or under a table. When the noise is prolonged, her fear becomes severe. She curls up into a ball and her teeth chatter. Sometimes during a thunderstorm, she will climb up on to my chair and wedge herself between my back and the chair. When Molly is fearful there is no use trying to comfort or distract her. She won't eat. She won't listen or obey us. Her "lizard brain" is in control.

Fear does that to us, too. When we are filled with fear, we are not capable of responding to God in a faith-filled way. We can't hear God's word to us. We are paralyzed and cannot risk taking a step. That means we can't live the life that he called us to when we are filled with fear. Imagine if Dr. Martin Luther King had been afraid of public speaking. He never would have stood in front of hundreds of thousands of people and declared "I have a dream!" We would have been robbed of one of the most impactful leaders in our nation's history. What if Thomas Edison had been afraid of failure? He would have quit conducting experiments that did not work, and the invention of the light bulb could have been delayed by years. We cannot live the life Jesus has called us to when we let fear have its way. What if the apostle Paul had been afraid of the opinion of others? He would never have been able to bring the Gospel to non-Jewish parts of the world. What if David had been afraid of Goliath? We cannot respond to fear and obey God's call at the same time. Not once in the New Testament does it say that Jesus was afraid.[41] Jesus did not fear, which is why he could live in constant communication and obedience to the Father.

Fueled by Imagination

Fear is faith in reverse. Faith is responding to God's word by envisioning it becoming reality. In contrast, fear imagines disaster becoming reality. The difference between fear and faith is often in what we imagine.

---

41 Jesus' sorrow and agony in the Garden of Gethsemane was a struggle to yield to God's will.

During the storm the disciples verbalized a clear mental picture of what they expected to happen: "We're going to drown!" (v. 25). They imagined the water overturning the boat and sweeping them under. They could envision themselves slipping under the waves and breathing water. To be fair, this was not a completely irrational idea under the circumstances. Luke's account of this event flatly states, "They were in great danger" (Luke 8:23). Many of the disciples were professional fishermen. They were aware of the danger of encountering a storm on the Sea of Galilee. No doubt they personally knew people who were drowned in the line of duty. The threat was not imaginary, but the outcome was. They were afraid because they imagined the worst.

Fear grows when we ask, "What if...?" and then provide a terrible answer to that question. When we imagine terrible things happening in the future, it causes fear. We should realize, though, that most of our fears never happen. We may imagine them, but ironically, they usually do not become reality.

I remember watching the New Year's Eve celebrations on December 31, 1999. The nation was tense with fear over 'Y2k.' Computer code written years before did not take the turn of the century into account, and many knowledgeable people believed that the nation's essential computer systems could malfunction at midnight January 1. People feared that we'd lose electricity, heat and running water. Some people even bought gas-powered generators and a year's supply of dry food because they were convinced that chaos would grip the nation. Fortunately, that fear was all wasted energy. None of that happened (due in part to action taken to prevent it). Since then, exaggerated fears have periodically gripped our nation, from Ebola to the Zika virus.

Five hundred years ago Montaigne said, "My life has been filled with terrible misfortunes, most of which never happened." Researchers have found that eighty-five percent of what subjects worried about never happened, and with the fifteen percent that did happen, seventy-nine percent of subjects discovered either they could handle the difficulty better than expected, or the difficulty taught them a lesson worth learning. This means that ninety-seven percent of what you worry over is exaggerations and misperceptions.[42]

Fear lies to us. It shrieks, "You are doomed!" Fortunately, that is not God's message to you.

Tell Yourself the Truth

"Do not fear" is easy to say but harder to do. How do we not fear when adrenaline is coursing through our veins and our minds are filled with worry? Since fear is fueled by imagining disaster, the solution is also found in changing our mental movie. Instead of envisioning a fear-inducing scenario, we need to picture what it will look like when God's word becomes reality. We expect that God's word to us is true and that it will happen. One of the ways we reinforce a mental image is by verbalizing what we are thinking.

Years ago, some parties I attended featured a game called Trivial Pursuit. The idea of this board game is to answer questions about often-obscure topics. It's a great game to play if you want to feel stupid. When we played the game in teams, there always came a moment when one member of the team would immediately offer the right answer, but then another teammate would step in and say, "Wait a minute, maybe it could be ..." and then make the case for a different answer. The team members would debate which answer was correct, going back and forth until finally guessing the wrong answer. As the one holding the answer card, it would be fun to watch them talk themselves out of the right answer.

We can also talk ourselves out of living by faith. What we tell ourselves, either inwardly or aloud, will shape our actions. It is hard to speak one way and act another. Imagine a football coach talking to his players in the locker room before a game, saying, "Look, you are not good enough to beat this team. They're bigger, faster and tougher than you. We all know we're gonna lose. Ready, hands in, say it together: 'We stink, we stink ...'" What if

---

42 http://www.huffingtonpost.com/don-joseph-goewey-/85-of-what-we-worry-about_b_8028368.html

at every practice the quarterback told himself, "I know I'm not good enough to win. I'm going to throw a bunch of interceptions. I'll probably fumble, too." Can you imagine that team going out and winning the game after talking like that? Now, just because a team says they're going to win doesn't mean they are going to do so. But repeatedly telling themselves they'll lose almost guarantees that they won't win.

If we dwell on mental images of defeat and disaster, we need not wonder why we feel anxious instead of faith-filled. It's hard to grow stronger in our confidence in God while constantly saying, "I'm afraid," "I can't," or "There's no way." To let faith overcome fear, decide your words will match God's truth. When we are feeling fearful, we can view that as a signal to starting telling ourselves what we know to be true about God. After all, why dwell on what is the exact opposite of what God said? When we feed our minds God's truth, faith grows and fear shrivels.

It's not that our words cause events, but our words impact us because we are likely to act in ways that are consistent with what we say. We can't do our best while imagining the worst. Our words can help us change the atmosphere of our minds.

In Psalm 42:5 the Psalmist deliberately adjusts his inner attitude by speaking to himself:

> "Why, my soul, are you downcast? Why so disturbed within
> me? Put your hope in God, for I will yet praise him, my
> Savior and my God."

The Psalm writer recognizes that he is feeling depressed and he decides to tell himself the truth about God. He exhorts himself to hope in God. He declares that he will praise the Lord again because he knows God promised to save his people. How different that Psalm would be if he had written, "My soul is downcast – and there is nothing I can do about it. Life is hard, and I'm afraid it won't get any better." I wouldn't want to pin that phrase on my computer monitor. Instead, the Psalmist engages the power of truthful speaking. We can do the same thing. Jesus is Savior, so let's speak like it that it is true. God is faithful, so let our words and thoughts reflect that faithfulness.

When worry or fear invades your heart, find a promise in the Scripture that speaks to that issue and repeat it to yourself regularly. For example, if you are getting anxious about money, you might repeat to yourself Jesus' words:

> "So do not worry, saying, 'What shall we eat?' or 'What shall we drink?' or 'What shall we wear?' For the pagans run after all these things, and your heavenly Father knows that you need them. But seek first his kingdom and his righteousness, and all these things will be given to you as well."
>
> Matthew 6:31-33

As you remind yourself of that promise, picture it becoming reality in your life. Let your imagination paint a mental picture of God meeting your need. Dwell on the way you will feel and the faithfulness of God.

Fear-Busting Affirmations

There are three biblical truths we can declare to ourselves in any situation. Reminding ourselves of these realities will fill our imaginations with faith-filled pictures. In fact, I have these three affirmations written on sticky notes and stuck on my bathroom mirror so that I can start every day by reading them.

Reality #1: Jesus Will Be There.

A few years ago, I came across a computer program that can edit people out of your pictures. For example, if you have a photo of your family on vacation and it includes your ex-spouse, you can edit out the person you don't want to see and keep the rest of the memory.

Fear edits Jesus out of our mental picture of the future. When we imagine an impending disaster, Jesus is nowhere to be seen. On the other hand, faith pictures Jesus with us in our future.

The disciples knew that storms on the Sea of Galilee had killed other fishermen. The main difference between those who were killed and the disciples was that Jesus was in the boat with the disciples. His presence changes everything.

That is what I learned when we were broken down on the side of the road in Mozambique. We drove as far as we could until the radiator boiled over and we had to stop. Then, we repeated the process of filling it with water and driving as far as it would take us. Finally, after an hour or so, we made it to a village. It was a proverbial wide spot in the road. There was no auto supply store in the area. In fact, there were no stores of any kind in that village. But there were some tables set up beside the road (think yard sale or flea market). Incredibly, there on one of those tables, sat a radiator cap that fit our old Toyota! For the second time that afternoon I thought, "How could this be happening?" This time, though, I wondered that with grateful relief. We paid whatever they asked, filled the radiator and headed for the city. In the meantime, we had been able to contact a missionary in the capital and he was on his way to pick us up. At that point we no longer needed a ride, so we formed a mini-convoy on the way back. We drove the last couple of hours in the dark, but I was too astonished by God's provision to be worried.

That experience taught me that when the worst thing happens, God will be there. It turns out that it was a lesson I was going to need. A few years later, I experienced several major, fear-inducing events in a short time span. Each event could have made my list of "worst things that could happen."

First, without warning, I had a cardiac arrest while working out at the gym. I was not overweight, my cholesterol was not high and I had little family history of heart problems. In fact, I had even passed a nuclear stress test a few weeks before. While running on a treadmill, I collapsed without a heartbeat. I ended up undergoing double by-pass surgery. Not long after that, our church's multi-million-dollar expansion project ran into problems and appeared to be on the verge of a disastrous shutdown. Each of the two main contractors was blaming the other for a major issue, and we were facing the possibility that work would stop and we'd be stuck with a half-done facility we couldn't use. Months after that, we had a significant shortfall in giving, even though atten-

dance was sharply higher. We had never had that kind of financial crisis before. Then, our family faced another serious crisis. A
few more major problems hit around the same time, and I became
concerned that the stress level was not good for a guy getting over
heart surgery.

In a short period of time, I faced several experiences that
would rank high on my list of "worst things." Yet somehow,
each one of those crises resolved very well. If I had made a list
of "worst things that could happen," cardiac arrest would have
ranked near the top. When it happened though, I found out that
God was there. After some amazing events, my heart is healthy
today. I later learned that only seven percent of people who have a
cardiac arrest outside of a hospital survive. Amazingly, not only
did I live, but I have no heart damage. I run three to five miles
several times per week with no trouble. Also, the building was
finished on time. When we were at the lowest ebb financially,
giving suddenly turned sharply up and stayed there without us
saying anything about it. The family crisis resolved in a positive
way, as did the other problems. I believe that through the car
breakdown in Mozambique, God was preparing and teaching me
a vital lesson that combats fear. He was saying, "When the worst
thing happens, I will be there."

No matter what happens in our lives, Jesus will be there. He
promised. Repeatedly.

- "Have I not commanded you? Be strong and courageous. Do
  not be afraid; do not be discouraged, for the LORD your God
  will be with you wherever you go" (Joshua 1:9**).**

- "And surely I am with you always, to the very end of the age"
  (Matthew 28:20).

- "God has said, "Never will I leave you; never will I forsake
  you" (Hebrews 13:5).

Faith is fed by picturing Jesus being active in our future.
Fear asks, "What if that happens?" and then imagines something
happening that we don't believe we can handle. Faith puts Jesus

in the picture by answering "What if ...?" with a confident, "Then Jesus ..."

As the disciples' boat was getting swamped, their fear screamed, "What if we sink and drown?" Nevertheless, Jesus was with them, and he commanded the storm to stop. They were saved.

When fear imagines, "What if ...?" faith answers with, "Then Jesus will give me the strength to face it." When there are rumors about layoffs at work fear asks, "What if I lose my job?" Faith answers, "Then Jesus will help me get a new one." Fear says, "What if I die?" Faith responds, "Someday it will happen, but then Jesus will be there to take me through and bring me to himself. Then I will experience more joy than I can imagine!"

When the worst happens, Jesus is there and he will act.

Reality #2: "Jesus is Greater Than This."

Not only will Jesus be present, he also has all power.

The disciples knew that Jesus was in the boat with them but they were terrified anyway. What they didn't realize was that Jesus' power was greater than the storm. They were shocked when they saw Jesus command the howling storm to stop, and then it did. They asked, "What kind of man is this?" Of course, today you and I know the answer to that question: "Jesus is the Son of God - creator of the universe. He's got all the power." That still wasn't clear to the disciples, however. They had seen him heal the blind and multiply the loaves and fishes. But their fear made them forget that. Besides, silencing a storm is a different degree of difficulty. If they had realized that Jesus had power over nature, perhaps they would not have become so terrified when the storm hit. They could have said, "OK, we have a problem here. We better ask Jesus to handle this."

You and I are not afraid of situations we can handle. Fear hits us when we don't think we can handle what's coming. For example: Let's say you have ten million dollars in the bank (humor me). One day the mechanic tells you that it will take five hundred dollars to repair your car. Are you going to lay awake at night worrying about that? No. You know that you have what it takes to take care of the need. On the other hand, let's say you have nothing in the bank, you don't get paid for another two weeks and your credit card is maxed out. Then, a five-hundred-dollar repair bill looks a lot different. You might worry about how you'll come up with the money and how you will get to work if you can't.

According to Amazon, the most highlighted passage in all books read on Kindle as of November 2014 — highlighted almost twice as often as any other passage — is one from the second volume of *The Hunger Games*. It reads, "Because sometimes things happen to people and they're not equipped to deal with them."[43] That's what causes fear in us: something is going to happen and I won't have the power to deal with it. The disciples discovered Jesus had power beyond what they ever imagined. Knowing that Jesus had that kind of power, they were no longer afraid.

When we are accosted by worry or face threatening situations, we can keep our imaginations healthy by reminding ourselves of the truth: Jesus will be there, and Jesus is greater than this. It doesn't matter what problem we face; Jesus is more powerful than that. Jesus has greater power than an illness or a job crisis. Jesus has more authority than those who threaten you, and he has the power to help you face the challenge in front of you. Whatever you will encounter today, you can truthfully say, "Jesus is greater than this."

The final affirmation you can make in the face of fear is:

Reality #3: "I Have Faith for This."

There is nothing that I will face that God will not give me the faith to handle. When we face a problem or worrisome future, we can say, "I have faith for this." God has given you all the faith you need to trust him for what you will face. You may not feel like you have sufficient faith, but you do. Just reach for it.

---

43 Mark Shiffman, *"Majoring in Fear,"* First Things (November 2014) Quoted in Preaching Today

Jesus said it only takes a little bit of faith to make a big difference. In Matthew 17:20 Jesus said, "I tell you the truth, if you had faith even as small as a mustard seed, you could say to this mountain, 'Move from here to there,' and it would move. Nothing would be impossible."

The disciples didn't have much faith, but they had enough to think to wake up Jesus. They had enough faith to turn to him. And that is all it took. God will give you enough faith to turn to him when you face something you can't handle.

As you listen for his word and envision his promise becoming reality, he will empower you to do what you need to do, even when you don't feel confident. He'll give you the strength to take the next step, the patience to wait, or the idea to act on. He'll give you boldness in prayer. He will connect you with people who will help you. God provides us what we need when we need it. Worry comes from trying to live tomorrow's problems with today's provision.

When fear threatens to strangle your soul, take control of your imagination. When it runs off into dark places, deliberately choose to picture the promises of God coming true in your life. Like the Psalmist, repeat the truths of God to yourself. Say it out loud if you need to convince yourself.

"Jesus is greater than this."

"Jesus will be there."

"I have faith for this."

Just weeks after my cardiac arrest, Pastor Dave Browning spoke at our church. Dave was a brilliant visionary who founded the Christ the King network of churches and wrote several helpful books on ministry and church multiplication. I wanted to spend some time with Dave when he was in town, but since I was recovering from heart surgery, I couldn't yet attend worship. I will always remember that after preaching three times on Sunday morning, Dave came to my house and sat at our dining room table patiently answering my questions until I had to lie down again.

A few years later, I was taken aback to learn that Dave had

been diagnosed with inoperable brain cancer at the age of 52. He handled the news with a calm trust. Shortly before Dave died, he reflected on his life with the clarity and perspective that impending death provides. He said, "Unless the hourglass gets flipped over, my time seems to be running out. I wish so much that I had not spent any of it complaining, or doubting, or worrying, or being afraid."[44]

Today we have the opportunity to fulfill Dave's wish for ourselves: live without fear.

---

44 *What Legacy Are You Leaving?* by Todd Wilson on Exponential.org

Chapter Seven Discussion Questions
Fear

1. Who is the most courageous person you know (or knew)? Why?

2. "Fear is faith in reverse?" How so?

3. What role has imagination played in your most recent fears? What are you imagining?

4. Which of these truths do you most need to focus on right now?
- Jesus will be there
- Jesus is greater than this
- I have faith for this.

5. What picture do you need to paint in your mind in order to free yourself from anxiety? Be specific.

CHAPTER EIGHT

Sin

A Step in the Wrong Direction

Obedience is an act of faith; disobedience is the result of unbelief.

— Edwin Lewis Cole

*When obedience to God contradicts what I believe will give me pleasure,
let me ask myself if I love Him.*

— Elisabeth Elliot

The whole town knew it was coming, but it was still spectacular when it happened. For years, the ground beneath the picturesque vacation house on the edge of a cliff in Texas had been slowly disintegrating. Water had been eroding the side of the cliff upon which the four-thousand-square-foot, $700,000 house stood, leaving it dangling over the lake below. The house was no longer safe to occupy. County officials watched the situation carefully, and finally decided it was time to take action. When a major storm drove everyone off the lake, fire officials took the opportunity to set the house ablaze and watched it tumble down the precipice into the water.[45]

A steady exposure to flowing water will eventually erode the foundation of a home and can lead to its destruction. Similarly, on-going exposure to sin in our lives will quietly eat away at the

---

45 Houston Chronicle, May 11, 2015 https://www.chron.com/news/houston-texas/texas/article/
Rain-soaked-cliff-where-burned-luxury-home-once-6255515.php

foundation of our faith. Left unchecked, unconfessed sin can even eventually lead to its tragic collapse. Unlike some kinds of soil erosion, though, spiritual erosion is entirely preventable.

Foundation for Life

Every one of us is imperfect and knows what it means to sin. We can be eternally grateful that we are saved by grace through faith,[46] and not by trying to earn God's acceptance by our own moral performance. At the same time, obedience to God's words is an essential component of developing a strong faith. Even when we do not understand the immediate results of our obedience, the fact that we have responded to God connects us with him more deeply. Each step of faith moves us closer to Jesus.

Sin, however, is a step in the wrong direction. When we get comfortable with ignoring what God says and following our own desires, we can expect doubt to start to crop up in us more frequently and more powerfully. We will have less desire to pray or to spend time in Jesus' presence. Our trust in God's goodness will dwindle. That is because faith is responding in trust and obedience to God's words. It is not primarily a feeling or a mere mental agreement to selected biblical propositions. The lives of the people listed in Hebrews 11 demonstrate that faith is a positive response to what God says. That means that faith in God and obedience to God are inseparably linked. That is exactly what Jesus taught.

In Luke 6:46 Jesus asked the penetrating question, "Why do you call me, 'Lord, Lord,' and do not do what I say?" The term "Lord" means top authority, the one in charge, the general, the CEO, in our terms. Jesus was asking a rhetorical question, "How can you call me the one in charge and not do what I say?" It doesn't make sense. To call Jesus, "Lord," means that he is in charge of our lives. Before we become followers of Christ, we do whatever we feel is best. When by faith we say, "Jesus is Lord," we are declaring that we will obey him.

---

46 Ephesians 2:8-9

Jesus went on to contrast two approaches to life:

"As for everyone who comes to me and hears my words and puts
them into practice, I will show you what they are like. They are like
a man building a house, who dug down deep and laid the foundation
on rock. When a flood came, the torrent struck that house but could
not shake it, because it was well built."

Luke 6:47-48

Jesus is saying that people who make it their practice to do
what he says will be glad they did. When life's hardships and
suffering strike like a flood, they will not fall apart. The essence
of their lives will hold; it won't give way. Faith will provide an
inner strength. People who regularly risk taking steps of obedience to do what they hear from God will deepen their trust in
him. Through experience, they learn that even when they don't
understand what is happening to them, they know God can be
trusted. Their faith will hold and they can maintain their spiritual balance.

Conversely, those who choose to ignore what Jesus says will
not have that solid foundation.

"But the one who hears my words and does not put them
into practice is like a man who built a house on the ground
without a foundation. The moment the torrent struck that
house, it collapsed and its destruction was complete."

Luke 6:49

The foundation of life is obedience to Jesus. Ignoring what he
tells us will not make our lives richer. It is called 'sin,' and it will
undercut the basis of our relationship with God, leaving our lives
vulnerable and our faith weaker.

I have spoken with a few people who said, "I tried God, but
it didn't work for me." Perhaps they were going through a tough
time in life when they heard that God had the answer, so they
prayed a prayer. Or, maybe they had an emotional moment when
they felt God's presence, and they realized they wanted God. Still,
their circumstances didn't quickly change in the way they had

hoped, so they walked away and did not follow Jesus. Maybe they never experienced the love, joy and peace they were promised, so they concluded that it was fictional. I want to explain to them that the transformed life they seek is real. Perhaps no one ever explained to them that the key to receiving it is to give God the steering wheel of their lives. They are right to look to Jesus in their time of pain; he will be our strength. However, God's abundant life comes when we follow Jesus, which means taking direction from him. Jesus is our Savior, and he is also our Lord.

To have faith in Jesus is to yield the leadership of our lives to him. The Apostle Paul led an incredibly adventurous and impactful life. He pioneered new churches, saw astonishing miracles, faced down riotous mobs and wrote much of the New Testament. It wasn't an easy calling. He was often pushed to the limit physically and emotionally. In Galatians 2:20 Paul shares a secret to his remarkable life:

> "I have been crucified with Christ and I no longer live, but Christ lives in me. The life I now live in the body, I live by faith in the Son of God, who loved me and gave himself for me."
>
> Galatians 2:20

By declaring, "I am crucified with Christ," Paul was essentially saying, "I used to call the shots in my life. I did what I thought was best. I made my own decisions. Now I don't do that. Now Jesus guides my actions and attitudes." That is what motivated his remarkable life.

Paul was quick to add, though, that his acceptance by God did not stem from his obedience. In the very next verse he said, "I do not set aside the grace of God, for if righteousness could be gained through the law, Christ died for nothing!" (Galatians 2:21). He knew that God saved him by grace, not because of his performance.

Corrosive Effects of Sin

Just because our best efforts at moral living cannot earn us salvation does not mean that obedience to God is irrelevant. After all, how can I follow Christ if I am going my own way? Telling Jesus, "I know what you want, but I am going to do what I want" is not a strategy for drawing closer.

If we want to grow in faith, we need to be aware of the reality that sin will undercut our ability to trust God deeply. There are multiple reasons that unconfessed sin erodes our faith and trust in God.

For one, choosing to sin makes us resistant the Holy Spirit's leading. In order to keep disobeying God, we have to learn to tune out the voice of the Holy Spirit who tells us, "No, that's not right." When we are about to choose to sin, often something in us says, "I shouldn't be doing this." Each time we go ahead and do it anyway, it becomes a little easier to ignore that voice the next time. When we rationalize our behavior and think up reasons why it is acceptable for us to do what God says not to, then we are no longer responding to God's words to us (which is the definition of faith). We cannot live a life of faith while tuning out the Holy Spirit.

Another reason sin erodes faith is that the guilt of disobedience increases a sense of distance between God and ourselves. Then we have less confidence in hearing, seeing and risking. We may even doubt that God is still for us. God's love for us does not change, but our response to him does.

When we hurt people, it usually damages our relationship with them.

Eighteen-year-old Taylor Smith was enjoying the afternoon with her good friend Jordan Holgerson atop a 60-foot-high bridge in Washington State. Jordan had seen a friend jump from the bridge and wanted to try it herself. She was in position at the edge of the bridge, but she was having trouble summoning the courage to step off. After words of encouragement didn't do the trick, Taylor shoved Jordan from behind, sending her sprawling into the air as she fell. When Jordan belly-flopped onto the water, the impact left her with six broken ribs, a punctured lung and air bubbles in her chest. Taylor was charged with reckless endangerment, which is punishable by up to a year in jail and a fine of $5,000. But the most enduring cost to Taylor may be the loss of her friendship with Jordan. After the incident, Taylor tried to visit Jordan in the hospital but was asked to leave. Taylor has not heard from Jordan since.[47] Taylor hurt Jordan, and that has damaged their relationship. Even though Taylor has apologized, Jordan cannot yet forgive her for what she did.

The bad news is that when we sin against God, we create distance between him and us. The great news is that when we ask for forgiveness from God, we don't have to wonder whether he will grant it; he promises that he will. That is a huge relief because we all need it.

The Grace We Need

Someday I will be done with sin. Unfortunately, today is not that day. As much as I hate to admit it, there are times I still do my will instead of God's will. I am pretty sure you didn't just faint over reading that. If we're honest, we will all say the same thing. 1 John 1:8 gives it to us straight, "If we say that we have no sin, we deceive ourselves, and the truth is not in us." The writer reminds us of the truth for an important reason. He is not giving us a license to shrug at sin and to dismiss our actions with, "Nobody's perfect." His motivation for writing it is to prompt us to deal with the reality of sin's effect on us.

God has provided us a way to keep sin from eroding the foundation of our faith. That is, to apply the great promise of 1 John 1:9, which is, "If we confess our sins, he is faithful and just and will forgive us our sins and purify us from all unrighteousness." As soon as we become aware that we have sinned, we can turn to God and confess it. To 'confess' means to tell God that we know that what we did was wrong, and to ask his forgiveness. This verse promises that when we do that, God forgives. That means there is no distance between us any longer. We have no more guilt, no more shame. Jesus died on the cross to pay the penalty for our sin so we don't have to. We are made completely right with our Heavenly Father.

---

47 https://abcnews.go.com/GMA/News/woman-pushed-teen-friend-off-bridge-admits-didnt/
story?id=57238510

God's forgiveness is complete; it covers all. There is nothing you have done that he cannot forgive. There is no limit on the times God will forgive you. Richard Sibbes said, "There is more mercy in Christ than sin in us." We don't need to make ourselves worthy of his forgiveness, it is by grace we are forgiven and saved. We don't deserve his forgiveness; he grants it out of his loving mercy.

Even more, 1 John 1:9 goes on to say that God will "purify us from all unrighteousness." Even though we may want to obey God, we find ourselves no match for sin. Our self-control is not enough. We need God's help and power in order to live for him. This verse tells us that God wants to provide that power to us. God goes beyond forgiving us for what we have done. He will also change us inwardly so that we do not have to keep falling into that sin. That process of inner transformation goes faster when we are growing in our faith.

The Good Life

Obeying God means a lot more than not breaking the rules, staying in line and not causing trouble. It's not just about adhering to a certain code of behavior. Obeying God is about learning to respond to his direction and guidance on a daily basis. That is the pathway to a rich and meaningful life.

If you feel spiritually stagnant or bored, here is a sure-fire recipe for reigniting your passion for Jesus: read the Bible and do what it says. Bible study can be good as long as it leads to action. Still, if we regularly read the Scripture and do nothing in response, we actually vaccinate ourselves against its message. If we consistently read God's truth, commands and promises, but do not let them impact our lives, we have successfully desensitized our souls to his words. After all, Jesus didn't die on the cross and rise again so that we could have good discussions on Wednesday nights. We need fewer Bible study groups and more Bible activation groups. Discussing the background and implications of a passage is fine, but if we want a stronger relationship with God, we need only to answer two basic questions: 1) What is God saying to me, and 2) What am I going to do about it? Then we go for it. That's where it gets interesting!

Clare DeGraaf says that the way to keep the flame of faith burning brightly in us over the long haul is to follow the "ten-second rule." In his book of the same name, Clare says the ten-second rule is simply this: "Just do the next thing you're reasonably certain Jesus wants you to do - and commit to it in the next 10 seconds before you change your mind."[48] What he is describing is a habit of instant obedience to God's voice. This is not legalism; it is liberating! Obeying God is not oppressive, it is the path to joy, peace and love. Yes, there will be difficult moments when we have to act against what we would naturally like to do, but there will be many more times of adventure and wonder as we see God at work.

Sam Miller is a member of our church who has been learning to say "Yes" to God on a consistent basis. Growing up, Sam went to church on Sundays, but he never made a connection with God. As a young man, Sam's life was filled with honest, hard work as a plumber, but also with anger, alcohol and other destructive habits. One Easter, he decided to attend a worship service. The sermon was one that he had heard before: "Build Your Life on the Rock of Jesus." For some reason, that day the message clicked. He realized he needed Jesus in his life. He made a commitment to follow Christ, and then started to learn more about what that meant. He began to read the Bible. He joined a small group and got to know other followers of Jesus. His life began to change in significant ways. His anger and combativeness faded away. He stopped drinking. He got married to his live-in girlfriend because he knew that's what God wanted him to do. He was building his life on the rock by doing what he heard Jesus telling him to do.

Sam soon heard about Jesus' call to "go make disciples." He learned how to tell the people around him about Christ. Eventually, he and a few other guys in his small group started going to an economically challenged area of town. They walked the streets and prayed for whoever they met. Sam found that people opened up to him when he told them, "I'm not a preacher, I'm a plumber." He and his friends prayed for addicts, prostitutes and

---

48 *The Ten Second Rule*, Clare De Graaf, (Howard Books, N.Y., N.Y.), 2013

lots of discouraged, broken people. Many had never heard anyone pray for them in their lives, and it deeply moved them. As Sam got to know the hurts and the needs of the people, Sam wanted to do more. He and the team gave away bicycles to kids who never had one before. They tried to show the love of Christ in practical ways.

One night Sam had a dream about a tent on the street with Bibles under it. So, he went out and bought a tent and a bunch of Bibles. He set up the tent in the middle of town and distributed Bibles to whoever wanted one. He also felt that God wanted him to help organize some outdoor evangelistic services in town. So he did. Hundreds of people attended, and dozens made decisions to follow Jesus. In fact, so many were moved by what they heard that a participating church in town was overcrowded the following Sunday with people at the altar seeking God.

Sam developed a habit of spending an hour each morning reading the Bible and praying. It is the primary way he hears from God, but the Lord also seems to speak to him through dreams from time to time. One night, Sam had another dream in which he saw a run-down storefront. He recognized it from the area of town in which they had been working. The next morning, Sam went to talk to the owner of the building. When he arrived, he was surprised to find the storefront vacant. He found the owner, who said, "Well, funny you should stop by - the place just went vacant three days ago." Sam leased the property on the spot.

Over the next few weeks, he and other volunteers worked to renovate the space with their own money. They opened it up to the community, calling it "The Good News Place." Sam envisions it as a place that forms a bridge between the church and the community, where people who would never go to a church can find friendship and hope in Christ. And that is exactly what is happening.

Just months after it has opened, it has become a hub of hope for the community. Sam now leads a men's group there on Tuesday nights. There's a group for high school students on Monday nights, Sam's wife leads a women's group Wednesday nights and his plumbing partner leads a Recovery group on Thursday nights.

The team uses a simple method of engaging the Bible, called Discovery Bible Study. It is comprised of a series of 6-8 questions that can be asked about any text. The goal is always the same, to challenge people to consider: What is God saying to me in this passage? What am I going to do about it?

Sam was concerned that this simple approach might seem uninteresting to anyone who was used to rigorous Bible Study. However, it has proved very effective in making disciples. The members have discovered that doing what the Bible says is a lot more exciting than just talking about it. For example, rather than simply reading about the Great Commission and discussing it, Sam invites guys to read the Great Commission and then go walk the streets with him and pray for broken people. That is not boring! It may be a little intimidating, but not dull! In fact, it is a transformational experience. Dozens of people have put their faith in Christ in the first few months of the center's existence. Did I mention that Sam is a plumber?

Sam is not only a changed man, he is also seeing God work through him to change others' lives. He has joy he never had before. He has a deep fulfillment that is unlike anything else. It is all because he has learned to say, "Yes" when God speaks to him. And because Sam says "Yes," he keeps hearing God speak more.

You may not be called to lease a storefront, but God has created you to reflect his glory. As you keep saying, "Yes" to his voice, you will step into the adventure of faith. Who knows what that will mean for you, but I can tell you this: it will be a lot more satisfying than sin.

Chapter Eight Discussion Questions
Sin

1. If you could live last week over again, what would you do differently?

2. Read Luke 6:46-49. Why is it impossible to be growing in faith and disobeying God at the same time?

3. Discuss Richard Sibbes' statement, "There is more mercy in Christ than sin in us." How does that give you hope?

4. What is the difference between a legalism that chokes life and a habit of obedience that gives life?

5. How does experiencing God's grace help us obey him more freely?

6. What blessing have you experienced from obeying God in a specific issue of your life?

CHAPTER NINE

Pain
Faith's Defining Moment

My flesh and my heart may fail, but God is the strength of my heart and my portion forever.

Psalm 73:26

Matt Davis used to be a devout Catholic who was so passionate about his faith that he would sometimes cry as he swallowed the Communion wafer.

Then came the Sandy Hook Elementary School massacre. A deranged shooter murdered twenty schoolchildren and six adults for no other reason but that they happened to be in the building. Matt said that when he saw news of that event, it was like a bell went off in his head, ringing, "There is no God, there is no God."

Matt is no longer a Christian. He frequently blogs and posts comments online under the name "Atheist Max." Some days he spends two or more hours online trying to argue people out of their religious beliefs in the comments section of online religious new stories.[49]

Matt's faith could not withstand the weight of pain.

A Defining Moment

Serious pain changes us. It upends our world and shakes us on a deep level. Ask parents whose child has died; they aren't the same. Talk to people who lost everything in the housing crisis;

---

49 https://religionnews.com/2014/12/01/online-troll-therapist-atheist-evangelists-see-work-calling/

they're different now.

But pain does not affect everyone the same way. Some people are crushed and broken by pain, yet others are not. I have known those who have endured true tragedy, yet still trust God deeply. And I have known others who have experienced far less pain who have discarded their faith.

Enduring a season of significant pain is like riding a bike up a hill; our faith will either go higher or fall backward. It won't remain where it is. True pain will not leave us the same way it found us. It can move us closer to God or further away from him.

What is it about pain that rattles our faith?

First, pain often raises questions we can't answer. As we saw in chapter six, questions are the raw material of doubt. The biggest (and oldest) question of all is, "Why?" When our bodies are wracked with pain or our lives turned upside down, we want to know the reason. How could a good God allow something so bad to happen to us or in our world?

A second reason pain can undermine our faith is that it can create fear, and fear is faith in reverse (see chapter seven). When pain hits us with no noticeable warning, we start looking for where it will strike again. We wait for the next shoe to drop. Focusing on potential threats keeps us from hearing and seeing God's word to us.

Also, pain can shatter our assumptions about the way life and God work. When that happens, faith is a casualty. For example, if we assume that God makes good things happen to good people, our trust in God will decline when the realities of life do not seem to bear that out.

The book of James starts with a message about suffering. The Apostle James wanted to help believers know how to respond to pain in a way that would strengthen and preserve their faith. This is what he said:

> "Consider it pure joy, my brothers and sisters, whenever you face trials of many kinds, because you know that the testing of your faith produces perseverance. Let perseverance finish its work so

that you may be mature and complete, not lacking anything. If any of you lacks wisdom, you should ask God, who gives generously to all without finding fault, and it will be given to you."

James 1:2-5

James tells us that pain is inevitable, but we can choose our response. There is a lot we cannot control: the genes we are born with, our country of origin or our family background. We can, however, choose how we respond to pain. Verse two tells us how to do that: "Consider it pure joy, my brothers and sisters, whenever you face trials of many kinds." Notice it says whenever you face trials, not if you face trials. We are all going to face trials at some point. They won't all be the same amount or the same variety, but they will come. Life will get hard. We might even suffer. We will experience trials "of all kinds" possibly including physical pain, injustice, grief or job loss, just to name a few.

I'm not trying to depress you. I'm trying to give you a heads-up so the trials will be easier to handle when they come. When I'm on a plane and the pilot tells us that we are approaching some turbulence, it's a lot easier to deal with the bouncing than if it is a surprise. I tell myself, "This is normal – it happens on flights. The pilot knew it was coming and is trained to deal with it." James is saying we'll have turbulence in life - it's normal. And the Pilot of our lives is fully capable of handling it.

The "Contract"

We need to hear James' word because many of us live with an unspoken, unexamined "contract" with God that goes something like this:

"I, the undersigned human being, will try my best to be a good person and to believe in God. In return, You the undersigned divine being will keep any really bad things from happening to me or to ones I love."

The assumed contract in a phrase is, "If we are good, God will give us a reasonably comfortable life."

If life goes the way we want it to go, that contract works for us. But at some point pain will find us. If it is intense enough, it will set off our inner alarm bells. Since we believe we have a contract with God, then one of two outcomes will result:

1. We will assume we have done something to deserve the pain. This will add guilt to our pain thus increasing our suffering.

   Or,

2. If we feel we don't deserve the pain, we will get angry with God for not fulfilling his contract responsibilities. Then we may become bitter. We will say something like,

   "God, I have always tried to serve you, why did you let my father/grandmother/child die?"
   "God, I have always been faithful in giving to you, how could you let me lose my job?"
   "Why did you let my spouse leave me?"
   "How could you let me get this disease?"

Faced with the reality that God has not held up his part of the contract, some will conclude that the only explanation is God does not exist. Many atheists came to reject God because they encountered pain and could not reconcile it with a loving God who didn't fulfill their contract.

Here's the problem with that contract: Jesus never signed it. He never promised to keep us from pain and suffering in exchange for our loyalty. In fact, he bluntly guaranteed us the opposite of comfort. In John 16:33 he said, "In this world you will have trouble. But take heart! I have overcome the world." Jesus told us we were going to have difficulty. None of us get to opt out of pain or trial, no matter how pleasing to God we are. And yet, we are not sentenced to a life of despair. Jesus assures us that he will prevail.

If anyone deserved a "no-suffering" contract from God, it was Jesus. But he ended up dying a torturous death on the cross. All but one of the apostles died violent deaths because of their faith in Christ. There was no protective contract for them, either.

The book of James was written to believers who knew that

suffering was part of the experience of following Jesus. In fact, the Church assumed this for centuries. Dr. Len Sweet wrote,

> "In his 6th-century commentary on the Book of Job, St. Gregory pointed out that the Lord's ways are very mysterious in that God sometimes allows good things to happen to good people. Yes, you read that right. It used to be disciples of Jesus, persecuted and mocked and martyred, expected the life of faith to involve suffering and sacrifice, and wondered what was going on when "the good times rolled." Today we've inverted the expectations and see suffering not as the norm but as the exception and the problem."[50]

Nik Ripken personally experienced more suffering than most people. He was an American missionary to Somalia during the great famine there in the 1990s. Moved by the plight of people who were dying by the thousands, Nik started a humanitarian organization that delivered desperately needed food to those who were starving. He confronted the agony of those starving to death and did what he could to save as many as possible. Since conditions were so bad, Nik's family lived in a neighboring country and Nik would fly in to Somalia to work.

Part of Nik's mission was to witness to the love of Jesus in that Muslim nation where Christianity was illegal. Late one night he secretly celebrated communion with four underground Christians he had discovered. Hours later, they were each found dead in different parts of the city. Later, Nik's teenage son died of an asthma attack due to a lack of basic medical care. If he had been back home in the United States, he would have lived. Because of his commitment to Christ, Nik chose to live and serve in one of the most desperate, violent places on earth with no thought to his own comfort. The evil was overwhelming. He dedicated himself to fulfilling the Great Commission, but none were converted. Four were murdered because of his attempt at ministry. He worked to save lives and it cost his own son's life.

The pain forced Nik off the mission field and led him to question most of what he believed about God. How could God be good

---

50 From a Facebook post by Len Sweet

when life was not? Tempted to give up his faith altogether, Nik instead set out to find answers. He traveled to sixty countries and interviewed hundreds of persecuted believers. Amazingly, he found people who were filled with joy in the darkness. He discovered that Jesus was enough.[51]

James 1:3 calls painful trials, "the testing of your faith." Under the pressure of pain, our faith will hold up and become stronger or it will weaken and possibly collapse. The book of James teaches us how to pass the test and emerge stronger than ever.

Choose to Let God Shape Us

God does not cause our pain, but he will use it to shape us into Jesus' image. James 1:3-4 says,

> "The testing of your faith produces perseverance. Let perseverance finish its work so that you may be mature and complete, not lacking anything."

God wants us to be mature and complete, and pain is one of the tools he uses to that end.

We become mature when we let perseverance do its work. People whose faith grows strong in trials choose to persevere through the pain, instead of escaping it.

A few of the ways we try to escape are:

- *Complain:* Listen to passengers react when a flight gets canceled or delayed. They don't realize they are giving up the benefit of that experience.

- *Lash out at others:* Hurting people hurt people. Often we take our hurt out on those closest to us. We're not letting perseverance do its work.

- *Run:* "I'm done; this isn't what I got married for ..." "I'm outta here ... I didn't sign up for this kind of aggravation ..."

When pain hits, sometimes God steps in and heals the disease, preserves the relationship or saves us from ruin. I love

---

51 Ripkin, Nik. *The Insanity of God.* Nashville,TN: B&H Publishing Group, 2013.

those moments! Jesus tells us to heal the sick and expect a miracle. Pray until the answer is "Yes." But for those times when the answer is "No," it is important to decide to persevere. If we don't give up, we will mature.

Ask What to Do

When we are hit by pain, we want to know why. God doesn't often tell us.

Sometimes there's a natural explanation. For example, if we don't study all semester, we shouldn't ask God why he let us flunk.

Other times, there is no easy answer to why we suffer, other than we live in a fallen world.

God doesn't tell us why, because he knows it wouldn't truly help us even if we knew. When parents lose a child, knowing "why" won't help them recover from the grief or trust God more deeply. They need to know what to do to make it through the day. They need to know what to do in order to handle their grief.

So instead of asking "Why?" we can ask God for wisdom for what to do.

James 1:5 says, "If any of you lacks wisdom, you should ask God, who gives generously to all without finding fault, and it will be given to you." When we are hurting, we can ask God to show us how to deal with what we are experiencing at that moment. He will not abandon us.

Notice Where God is Working

David underwent surgery to remove much of his colon. While recovering in the hospital, he was physically weak and worried about whether the tissue removed during the surgery would be cancer. He was a colon cancer survivor, and for years wondered whether it would return.

The doctor said test results would take two weeks or so. As he lay awake one night, he prayed. He was worried about test results and asked for courage to wait.

The next day, the doctor who had treated him after his colon cancer surgery years before made an unexpected visit. She said that she had happened to see his pathology results and wanted to assure him that there was no evidence of cancer. David was amazed and relieved.

He said, "God spoke his love into my fears and answered the one question that was troubling me. I cried when she gave the report and no one there really knew why." David had seen God at work in his pain, and it made all the difference.

If we dwell on asking, "Why?" we will miss the encouragement that comes from God reaching out to us. Seeing God at work encourages us and builds our trust in him.

God will be at work in your pain. It is a promise from God himself.

Romans 8:28 says, "And we know that in all things God works for the good of those who love him, who have been called according to his purpose."

This doesn't say that God causes bad things to happen. It doesn't say that everything works out for the best. It says that even when bad things happen, God can take them and turn them into something good, like an artist taking junk and turning it into a masterpiece. There is no pain in your life that God can't make work for good in your life. "In all things God works for the good of those who love him." ALL THINGS. That means God never wastes a hurt.

Look Toward Eternity

The character Han Solo is one of the heroes in the *Star Wars* movies. At the end of *The Empire Strikes Back,* Han is captured by the bad guys and frozen in carbonite. His anguished face fills the screen, and the movie ends a few minutes later. It was a somber ending. But every Star Wars fan knew that it wasn't really the end for Han. Everyone knew there was another movie to come. There was hope. Sure enough, in the sequel Han was rescued from his frozen state.

If you are in an episode of pain, remember that there is a

sequel coming to your story. The story is not done this side of heaven. James 1:12 says, "Blessed is the one who perseveres under trial because, having stood the test, that person will receive the crown of life that the Lord has promised to those who love him."

If this life is all there is, there may be no reason for joy in suffering. If this is it, then injustice wins. Sickness robs us of life.

But this life is not all there is! Injustice does not get the final word, Jesus does. The pain we endure shapes us for future glory!

Nancy and her husband were a pastoral team. After years of leading churches, they dedicated themselves to planting new churches throughout their region. For decades, they worked long hours, often in obscure places, to establish new churches in places that needed them.

One day her husband did not come home as usual. Without warning, he had died of a heart attack. He was only in his early fifties. Nancy was crushed. Both her partner and her job were gone. Her pain was deep. She missed her husband and their life together so much it hurt. However, her life was built on the rock of obedience to Jesus, and her faith held.

Several years later, Nancy remarried. Her life began to open up again as she became part of a new family. She joined our church and gained a fresh vision for making a difference. Life was good again.

Then came the diagnosis: cancer. Her days filled up with doctor appointments and chemotherapy treatments. Even so, Nancy was filled with hope and was constantly smiling. Most weekends, she tracked me down to tell me about the patients and doctors she prayed for at her chemo sessions. I called her a missionary to the cancer center.

We continued to pray fervently for Nancy's complete healing. Many of us believed that Nancy had more of the race to run and that she would make a kingdom difference for years to come. There were several hopeful signs that seemed to confirm this.

The doctors tried new approaches in search of healing, but

to our surprise, her hopes were dashed each time. The disease progressed.

When it became clear that God's answer to our prayers was "no," she agreed to be interviewed on video so she could share with the whole church what she was learning. She said, "My body is dying, but I'm not. I marvel at the journey … me and my God. He gave me a profound joy nestled deep in my soul that went above the cancer. It shows the greatness of my God and the support of numerous precious people who encouraged and prayed for me. Yes, I feel blessed and full of joy for all. Amazingly, there is joy in my cancer."

Nancy's funeral service was a celebration of God's goodness and her eternal perspective.

The Apostle Paul endured a lot of suffering and loss for the cause of Christ. Listen to his perspective, "I consider that our present sufferings are not worth comparing with the glory that will be revealed in us" (Romans 8:18).

All pain is temporary. Life with God is forever. And the character we develop through temporary suffering here will last forever with God. James 1:12 says, "Blessed is the one who perseveres under trial." Why blessed? "That person will receive the crown of life that the Lord has promised to those who love him."

Pain will test our faith, but it is not a sign that there is something wrong in our relationship with God. Those Hebrews 11 heroes will attest to that:

> "Some faced jeers and flogging, and even chains and imprisonment. They were put to death by stoning; they were sawed in two; they were killed by the sword. They went about in sheepskins and goatskins, destitute, persecuted and mistreated— the world was not worthy of them. They wandered in deserts and mountains, living in caves and in holes in the ground. These were all commended for their faith, yet none of them received what had been promised, since God had planned something better for us so that only together with us would they be made perfect."
>
> Hebrews 11:36-40

Chapter Nine Discussion Questions
Pain

1. Some people lose their faith through pain, others come through pain with a stronger faith. What is the difference?

2. What is wrong with the "contract" that provides God's protection from pain in exchange for good behavior?

3. How has God shaped you through a time of pain?

4. Why is an eternal perspective essential for handling pain in a way that builds faith?

5. In what way are you wrestling with pain right now? Where do you see signs of God at work in the situation?

Part Three

Living
it

CHAPTER TEN
It Takes a Community

"Show me your friends and I'll show you your future."

—Anonymous

A commemorative plaque stands outside a picturesque stone cottage in Eyam, Derbyshire, England. It is a grim reminder of the last time the Great Plague ravaged England and of the human toll it exacted. The plaque reads:

> **"Nine members of the Thorpe family lived here.**
>
> **They all died.**
>
> **Thomas Thorpe died 26th September 1665**
>
> **Mary, his daughter, died 30th September 1665**
>
> **Elizabeth, his wife, died 1st October 1665**
>
> **Thomas, his son, died 20th December 1665**
>
> **Alice, his daughter, died 15th April 1666**
>
> **Robert, his son, died 2nd May 1666**
>
> **William, his son, died 2nd May 1666**
>
> **William and Mary Thorpe the parent of Thomas senior died 166** [sic]."

It is hard to imagine the horror and pain the Thorpe family endured as they watched one another sicken and die.

Incredibly, they were not surprised that it happened. In the summer of 1665, the town's tailor took delivery of a bolt of cloth from London. When it arrived, it was damp. So, the tailor spread the cloth out in front of his fireplace. He did not realize that it contained fleas carrying the plague. Within a week he was dead.

When the town realized that the plague had come to Eyam, the pastor called a meeting. The people knew that bubonic plague was highly contagious and that their best hope of survival was to flee. But they accepted the fact that if they left, they would only spread the infection throughout England. So, persuaded by their pastors, they voted to stay. They quarantined the village; no contact with humans outside the village was allowed. Over the next fourteen months, nearly half the town died; but the surrounding regions were spared.

Contagious Faith

Bubonic plague was highly contagious and usually fatal. Faith in Jesus can also be highly contagious. However, it is always life-giving! When we hang around people who have faith, we are likely to catch it ourselves – and be thankful that we did.

The people around us influence us. If you don't believe me, look at your clothing. I would be very surprised if you were wearing a Roman toga or large buckles on your shoes like a Pilgrim. We wear what the people around us wear. My kids laugh at my high school picture because I am wearing bell-bottom jeans with my hair down to the shoulders. Why did I dress that way? Because everyone else did! In my wedding picture, I am wearing glasses with oversized frames. That was the style then! We can sometimes date a picture by the clothes the people are wearing. If we see a woman with linebacker-sized shoulder pads and big hair, we say to ourselves, "That's the 1980s!"

It is not just our clothing choices that are influenced by the people around us. Others can also shape our moral values and our convictions about what is true.

Social psychologist Solomon Asch conducted a famous experiment about the great power of peer pressure. He showed groups of college students drawings of a line and then asked each student to identify which of several other lines matched it in length. The answer was obvious. However, all the students except one were secretly working in league with Asch. The lone exception was one unwitting test subject.

Asch instructed all his confederates to answer some trials correctly. For some prearranged trials, though, they were to insist that a shorter (or longer) line was the correct match. He wanted to investigate what individuals will do when confronted with a group that declares that "wrong" is "right." Not surprisingly, nearly 100 percent of his subjects picked the correct line when choosing on their own. But when the group was insisting on the wrong answer, 3 out of 4 subjects betrayed their own judgment and sided with the majority at least once. In fact, nearly 4 in 10 sided with the group and responded wrong every time.[52] Asch showed that human beings are willing to ignore reality and declare what is wrong to be right in order to conform to a group.

It is extraordinarily difficult to stay confident about what we believe when others around us are declaring opposing ideas. That is one reason we can't grow in faith on our own.

Faith is a trusting response to God's words to us. We, however, live in a culture that is not based on following Jesus. We are bombarded daily with messages that run counter to what God's word says. We are only fooling ourselves if we think that we can consistently generate the confidence needed to envision and risk acting on God's word when most people around us are declaring it wrong or irrelevant.

Sadly, many American Christians today view spiritual growth as a solo activity. One out of three Christians says they prefer to pursue spiritual growth on their own rather than with others. Two in five of all Christian adults consider their spiritual life to be "entirely private."[53]

This attitude takes a toll on our faith. Researcher George

---

52 from *Peer Pressure,* by Katherine Kersten, posted April 4, 2011 https://www.americanexperiment.org/article/peer-pressure/

53 *New Research on the State of Discipleship* - Barna. posted Dec. 1, 2015 https://www.barna.com/research/new-research-on-the-state-of-discipleship/

Barna found that when dealing with doubt, Christians who turned away from the church and their believing friends said that doubt was destructive to their faith. Believers who turned to friends, family or the church when they faced doubt, however, said that they emerged from that season with a stronger faith than before.[54]

Hebrews 10:24-25 spoke to this reality long ago, giving us the key to staying spiritually strong over the long haul:

> "And let us consider how we may spur one another on toward love and good deeds, not giving up meeting together, as some are in the habit of doing, but encouraging one another—and all the more as you see the Day approaching."

The heroes listed in Hebrews 11 were not isolated in their faith journeys. Each made individual choices to hear, see and risk responding to God, but they lived out those choices in relationship with others. Abraham and Sarah had their extended household, Noah pursued God's purposes along with his family while Gideon gathered an army that would risk obeying God with him.

We cannot mature fully in our faith simply by reading our Bibles in the privacy of our own homes. We need to connect with other people. We need community.

Becoming a Spiritual Family

As soon as the Church was born it became a spiritual community.

Before the risen Jesus ascended to heaven, he told his followers to go wait for the Holy Spirit to fill them. They did, and about ten days later the Holy Spirit came upon them in such a noticeable way that crowds gathered. The Apostle Peter then preached about the resurrection of Jesus, and 3,000 were converted. The next day, those new converts gathered together again. And the day after that. And the day after that.

---

54 *Two-Thirds of Christians Face Doubt* - Barna posted July 25, 2017 https://www.barna.com/research/two-thirds-christians-face-doubt/

Acts 2:42 says, "They devoted themselves to the apostles' teaching and to fellowship, to the breaking of bread and to prayer." They devoted themselves to four community-based practices, including "fellowship." That meant that they weren't devoted only to meeting, they were devoted to each other.

Those early believers became a family. You can tell they were a family because they started calling each other "brother" and "sister." This was the first time in history that God's people referred to each other this way. When the original disciples followed Jesus throughout Israel for three years, they didn't call each other "brother." I find no record in the Old Testament of Jews calling each other "brother" or "sister" unless they were physically related. But God's people started doing so after the Holy Spirit was given and the Church was born.

One such example is in Acts 9. Paul was on his way to destroy the church when the risen Jesus appeared to him. At that moment he changed from being a persecutor of the church to being a member of the church.

> "Placing his hands on Saul, [Ananias] said, "***Brother*** Saul, the Lord—Jesus, who appeared to you on the road as you were coming here—has sent me so that you may see again and be filled with the Holy Spirit"
>
> Acts 9:17

You probably don't want to know what the believers called Saul while he was arresting and killing Christians. But as soon as he had his vision of Jesus, other believers called him "Brother." He became part of the family.

Just as we are born physically into a human family, we are born spiritually into God's family. John 1:12 says, "Yet to all who did receive him, to those who believed in his name, he gave the right to become children of God." The moment anyone puts their faith in Jesus, they become children of God. That means God is now their heavenly Father. If God is my father, and God is your father, that makes us brothers (and sisters). We are not meant to live as only children.

I've always said there are at least two things you can't do on your own: one is to get married, and the other is to follow Jesus. That is because the nature of both involves other people. Following Christ is a group activity. To say, "I want to be a Christ-follower but I don't want to be part of a spiritual community" is like saying, "I want to be a football player but I don't want to be part of a team." It can't be done.

There are over fifty "one another" statements in the New Testament with exhortations like:

- love one another (1 John 3:11)

- forgive one another (Colossians 3:13)

- encourage one another (2 Corinthians 13:11)

- accept one another (Romans 15:7)

- be patient, bearing with one another (Ephesians 4:2)

- honor one another (Romans 12:10).

If we are going to obey these Spirit-inspired instructions, we need to be in community with one another. How can we bear one another's burdens if we don't know what they are? How can we encourage one another if we don't know when they are discouraged – or if we don't know their telephone number to call or text them?

There are many different forms of Christian community: traditional church, house church, small group, mission team and so on. And we each have our own preferences as to which is best, which is fine. We can grow spiritually in any one of them, as long as it promotes personal connection with other believers. The point is that in order for our faith to thrive, we need to be in community with others.

Share in Common

Acts 2:42 says that the first believers were devoted to "the fellowship." Today, "fellowship" has become a churchy code word for "drinking coffee after worship." But it meant a lot more to the early church.

The word "fellowship" comes from the word meaning "common" which is the root of our words "communion" and "community."

Acts 2:44 says, "And all who believed were together and had all things *in common*." The first believers became a family because of what they had in common. And what was that? The next few verses tell us.

First, they shared *a common faith.*

Verse 44 says the community was made up of "all who believed." First and foremost, they each had turned from sin and received forgiveness and new life from Jesus.

When you meet someone who had the same life-altering experience as you did, there is a bond. For example, people who went to the same college and were members of the same fraternity sense a bond as soon as they meet. They share a life-shaping experience. The first believers shared the experience of being saved from a meaningless life and being filled with the Holy Spirit.

Second, they shared *a common commitment to care for each other.*

Acts 2:45 says, "And they were selling their possessions and belongings and distributing the proceeds to all, as any had need." The early church took care of one another in real ways. That's what a healthy family does. When one member is in need, the others don't say, "It's tough to be you – good luck." No, they look for a way to help.

We may not regularly sell our possessions to help those in our small group, but let's not avoid the challenge of the early church's example. In 1 John 3:17 the apostle John wrote, "Whoever has the world's goods and sees his brother in need and closes his heart against him, how does the love of God abide in him?" We're called to care for one another in practical ways.

Third, the early church had *a common commitment to seek God.*

Acts 2:46 reads, "Every day they continued to meet together

in the temple courts. They broke bread in their homes and ate together with glad and sincere hearts."

These believers went to the temple together as a large group. They didn't stay home and say, "I can pray privately." When the Spirit of God fills people, they worship together. The early church also got together in their homes in a small group setting. They sought God together in groups of all sizes.

Our community is based on what we have in common. At the same time, it is worth noting what the disciples in the early church did not have in common. Acts 2 tells us these believers were from all over the world. That meant that they did not share a common language, culture, race or government allegiance. Yet, they had a deep sense of community because what they shared in common was more powerful than their differences.

That is the beauty of the local church. Our unity does not stem from our similarities. We have community in the midst of diversity because what we have in common is more important than our differences.

The next time you are in a Wal-Mart, look around and notice whom you see. (Yes, I know there are "People of Wal-Mart" websites.) When you are in Wal-Mart, the people you see are the people who make up your community. You might notice some people who you didn't even realize lived near you. Our churches should look like our Wal-Marts. I don't mean they are to be laid out in aisles. I mean that they should be made up of the variety of people who live in our community. We are called to make disciples of all people.

Are you in community with people who share a common faith? Are you part of a spiritual family that is committed to caring for one another and that is devoted to seeking God together? If you are, there is a good chance that your faith is healthy.

Medical researchers found that if a friend of yours becomes obese, you are nearly 50% more likely to gain weight yourself. They also found that if your friend smokes, you are over 60%

more likely to smoke. Happy friends make you happier, too.[55] Should it be any surprise, then, that our closest friends will either help or hinder us in hearing, seeing and risking obedience to God? If we want to grow in our faith and make the rest of our lives count, we absolutely need to be part of an authentic Christ-centered community. Here are a few steps toward building it.

Practice Loving Fellow Followers

Christ-centered community is what results when people love one another. That is what we're called to do! In Romans 12:10 the Apostle Paul says, "Be devoted to one another in love." When we are committed to listening to others, meeting their needs, showing patience with them and celebrating their strengths, community is the valuable by-product.

Loving one another was Jesus' great commandment. He told us,

"A new command I give you: Love one another. As I have loved you, so you must love one another. By this everyone will know that you are my disciples, if you love one another."

John 13:34-35

The Old Testament contained hundreds of laws about which festivals to keep and how to keep them, what to eat, how to keep the Sabbath and so on. Jesus updated all those laws. He told us there is really only one law, and that is to love one another. Love fulfills the law because if we love people, we won't kill them. If we love people, we won't steal from them or lie to them. When we focus on loving others, we stay in the center of God's will. Christ-centered community is the result of loving others. It is also an ideal environment for practicing love toward others.

In order to practice this kind of "one another" love, we need to get to know others beyond a surface level. We need more than a shoulder-to-shoulder experience on Sunday morning. We need the face-to-face relationships that can develop in small groups or

---

55 https://medium.com/the-mission/youre-not-the-average-of-the-five-people-you-surround-yourself-with-f21b817f6e69

missional communities.

Al and Teresa have led small groups at our church for decades. They said, "We do life together – weddings, funerals, births. We eat in or out together. We pray for each other and see answers. They come as strangers and we love them like family."

Loving others is more than a vague feeling of goodwill or trying to be "nice." It is putting others' interests ahead of our own, listening, encouraging and more. Ask God for the power to practice loving fellow followers and you will build community.

Share Your Life

Community involves sharing the fullness and reality of our lives. It is possible to be in each other's company and still not truly connect. Much of the time, we present only a Facebook version of ourselves to others. That is, we let people see the edited highlight reel of our lives; the good stuff that we are proud of. Much of the time, that is fine. In fact, it is not wise to reveal publicly our unfiltered thoughts and experiences where strangers with bad motives can take advantage of us.

Fortunately, in a healthy family, you can be who you are. If we are going to experience true community, we need to let people behind the wall we put up to the rest of the world. If we never let anyone see who we are, the good news is that we won't be hurt as often. The bad news is that you will lose out on what it means to love and be loved. You won't know the power of knowing others and being known. To step into community, at some point we need to take the risk of being real with others. The rewards are worth it.

Joseph and Angela Johnson are group leaders at our church, and they have experienced the power of Christ-centered community. A couple of years ago they concluded that God was leading them to adopt a child from China. They were excited about it, but they knew that it is a very expensive process. Since they live in community, they shared this decision with several of the small groups they helped to start. Before the Johnsons knew it, those group members planned a drive-in movie night fund-raiser for them. And when the Johnsons later organized a fund-raising race, those same small groups all participated and volunteered at the event. For a solid year, the group members cheered on Joseph and Angela as they raised money.

Then came the hardest part: waiting for a match. For over a year the Johnsons waited as agencies tried to connect them to the right child. Angela said, "I admitted to several of my best group friends that I wasn't really sure how to keep praying. I felt like such a broken record. But these women banded together and created the most lavish of letters and cards with prayers in them. When I didn't have the words, they did. They arranged for coffees to be delivered to my work multiple times. My secretary asked, 'How do you have such nice friends?' I told her, 'They are from my small group.'"

Finally, the Johnsons were matched to a little girl. The night they all arrived back from China, their group set up luminaries in their neighborhood. They were surrounded by meals and support for weeks. Angela said, "Our whole community is seeing Jesus' hands and feet through these families. I have had so many people say to me, 'Wow you have a great support group.' And we do, because of small group – because Jesus is at the center of our relationships!"

When you get real with people, you will encourage others, and you will find a new level of support in your journey toward where God is calling you. You will be inspired to keep trusting Christ, and you will impact others. And when you are in true community with other Christ-followers, their faith will rub off on you.

Protect your Relationships

Just as there is no such thing as a perfect family, there is no perfect church or community. Sometimes we picture an idealized image of the early church. However, they had their issues and problems. Read the letters of Paul, James and John in the New Testament and you will see the early church had conflict, immoral behavior and power struggles. We have those letters in the Bible because the apostles had to deal with issues in the church!

Life in Christian community is rich and fulfilling. At the same time, when we get close to each other in our spiritual family we will see their imperfections. We will rub each other the wrong way. We might even hurt each other or have conflict. We can be like porcupines on a cold night. We need to come together to survive, but when we do, we poke each other.

Relationships take maintenance. That is why the Lord gives us instructions on dealing with the inevitable problems that arise. We are told:

1. *Pray for one another,* especially for those who offend or hurt you.

This is a great way to inoculate your community against the virus of disunity. In his classic book *Life Together,* Dietrich Bonhoeffer writes, "I can no longer condemn or hate a brother for whom I pray, no matter how much trouble he causes me."

2. *Go directly to anyone who hurts you.*
In Matthew, Jesus said,

> "If your brother or sister sins, go and point out their fault, just between the two of you. If they listen to you, you have won them over. But if they will not listen, take one or two others along."
>
> Matthew 18:15-16

Jesus said that if someone in your community hurts you, tell everyone you know what the fool did. No, that's not it. Jesus told us to go directly to the person who hurt you and work it out! Don't run away. Don't talk to other people about the issue. Go right to the person involved and work it out. If you can't resolve the issue that way, bring in a mature Christ-follower who can help. This principle keeps conflict clean and prevents the infection of bitterness from spreading through a community.

Charles Spurgeon said, "One log does not burn well by itself." And our faith does not burn brightly for long when removed from the fireplace of community. It takes effort to build Christ-centered relationships, but it is worth it!

Chapter Ten Discussion Questions
It Takes a Community

1. Share a time you followed a fad that seems silly now (clothing, music, activity, etc.)

2. "There are at least two things we can't do on our own: get married and follow Jesus." Would you agree or not? Why?

3. In what ways have other believers influenced your faith? Be specific.

4. What does it mean to be in community with other believers? (Acts 2:42-47).

5. Why is it vital to let yourself be truly known by another Christ-follower?

6. What step(s) would be required for you to deepen your community with a few other believers?

Know it

"Blessed assurance, Jesus is mine,
O what a foretaste of glory divine."

— Fanny Crosby

"It is possible for a man to know whether
God has called him or not. ... if you anxiously
desire to know, you may know."

— Charles Spurgeon

"Fake news" became a tired buzz phrase after the 2016 U.S. election. Let's pull the term out of the highly charged world of politics and have a little fun with it. Let's see if we can spot the fake (non-political) news. Try to guess which of the following headlines are real and which are fake ones taken from satire sites.

1. River Rat Burger All the Rage in Russia[56]

2. New Report Finds Americans Most Interested in Science When Moon Looks Different Than Usual[57]

3. Discovery of Prehistoric Corn Chips Turns Paleo Diet on its Ear[58]

---

56 True, but no mention of the recipe http://www.nbcnews.com/video/-river-rat-burger-all-the-rage-in-russia-818270787586

57 Fake: it's from the satirical website The Onion

58 Fake; Cave men didn't do guacamole dip either.www.cap-news.com/section.php?id=health#sthash.189JCDdp.dpuf

4. New Halloween App Lets Kids Trick or Treat from Safety of Home[59]

5. Oregon Man Changes Name to Captain Awesome [60]

6. Candidate's wife says 'Re-elect him before he drives me crazy.[61]

So, what do you think? Which are the real headlines and which are made up? (The answers are in the footnotes.)

It can be fun to try our hand at picking out the fake headlines from the true ones because it doesn't really matter whether we guess right or not. Whether or not there is actually a guy whose legal name is Captain Awesome will make no difference to our lives – unless you choose to marry him and become Mrs. Awesome.

But fake news about how we are made right with God, now that's a different matter. Being misled about getting right with God can lead to us missing out on the abundant and eternal life Jesus offers.

That explains why the Apostle Paul wrote such a passionate, forceful letter to the believers in the region of Galatia. Someone was giving the Galatians fake news about how to find peace with God, and lives were at stake.

A few years before, the Apostle Paul and his team visited the region of Galatia, which is in modern-day Turkey. They met people who sincerely wanted to know God, so he and his team shared the Gospel with them. The word "gospel" literally means "good news." 1 Corinthians 15 says the Gospel is the good news that Jesus died to pay the price for the sins of the world, then rose again three days later. Today, Jesus offers new life to anyone who

---

59   Fake; That might happen someday, but not yet! http://www.cap-news.com/section.php?id=tech#sthash.fVDNjjlU.dpuf

60   True; I guess he wanted people to think of him every time they said, "That's awesome."http://content.usatoday.com/communities/ondeadline/post/2010/12/oregon-man-changes-name-to-captain-awesome/1#.WITClrYrJzg

61   True; Charlyn Daughtery made a commercial asking Texas voters to give her husband Gerald something to do and get him out of the house. And he won! http://www.today.com/video/texas-candidate-s-wife-to-voters-re-elect-him-before-he-drives-me-crazy-793891395531

puts their trust in him.

The Galatians believed this good news to be true, and they turned to follow Jesus. They were amazed and grateful that their sins had been forgiven when they put trust in Christ. They were excited to know they were God's children and would live forever with him. They stopped worshiping idols and began loving Jesus and each other. A new and thriving church was born.

A little later, trouble started. Some teachers came from Jerusalem and started spreading fake good news, a false gospel. They told the Galatians that believing in Jesus was great, but that if they really wanted to be accepted by God, they also had to keep the Jewish ceremonial laws. They had to stop eating meat from the markets and start eating only kosher foods. They had to start observing the Jewish festivals. They had to get circumcised. In other words, they had to become Jewish. After all, Jesus was the Jewish Messiah.

Sadly, the Galatians believed this fake good news. Admittedly, these preachers were from Jerusalem, which is where Jesus rose from the dead and where the apostles lived. And the messengers sounded very authoritative. They were very confident they were right.

When Paul heard about this he was alarmed and angry. He was in another country starting more churches, so he dashed off a letter to warn the Galatians that they were following fake good news and being led further away from God instead of toward him. Paul wrote,

"I am astonished that you are so quickly deserting the one who called you to live in the grace of Christ and are turning to a different gospel— which is really no gospel at all. Evidently some people are throwing you into confusion and are trying to pervert the gospel of Christ."

Galatians 1:6-7

Paul was blunt. He told the Galatians that they were deserting truth and believing a fake gospel. He said those visiting preachers were perverting the Gospel. That is, they took the true good news, and they twisted it out of shape so that it was no longer good news. These teachers were called "Judaizers" because they were trying to make the Galatian believers live like Jews.

Fake Good News

You and I will hear fake good news today, too. We will hear messages about how to find peace with God that sound plausible but are not completely true. They are twisted versions of the real good news of Jesus.

Here are a few of the common versions of fake good news we hear today:

Fake Good News: To be accepted by God, try to be a pretty good person.

Maybe you've heard people say, "I think I'm good with God because I try not to hurt people. I do what I can to help out where I can. I've never murdered anyone and I'm kind to animals. Compared to most people I'm a pretty decent person."

That line of thinking is based on the assumption that good people go to heaven and bad people don't. It supposes that at the end of my life, I'll stand before God, and if I have done more good than bad, I'm in.

This is a very common idea. It appeals to our senses of fairness. But it is fake good news. It's not the "real" good news of the Gospel. And, it is not good news at all.

For one thing, it leaves us uncertain. How high is the bar for entrance into heaven? How good do I have to be in order to be accepted by God? How do I know whether I have made the cut, or not? I can never be sure. That's why when you ask some people if they are going to heaven they'll say, "I hope so ..." There is no way to know.

What does it mean to be "good" anyway? Good compared to what or who? Compared to a serial killer? OK, I'm better than that. Compared to Mother Teresa? I'm not as good as her. What's the standard? If we don't know now, it will be too late later.

The Bible says that for God the standard of goodness is not other people, it is God himself. And God is perfect, but none of us are (not even Mother Teresa). So, we assume that God will grade on a curve. But will he? How do we know?

The problem with the assumption that good people go to heaven is that, compared to God, there are no good people. Romans 3:12 says, *"There is no one who does good, not even one."* None of us can be good enough, because the standard is God, and none of us measure up. Romans 3:23 tells us, "All have sinned and fall short of the glory of God."

It is not good news to paralyzed persons that they will be loved if they run a 5k. That is cruel, because they can't do it. And it is not good news to tell morally imperfect people like us that God will love and accept us if we're good people. That is not the good news of the Gospel.

Fake Good News: "To be accepted by God, believe and be religious."

This is the distorted gospel the Galatians fell for. They were told, "If you want to be saved, believe in Jesus and keep the Jewish religious laws." The Judaizing preachers told them that God would accept them if they kept the Jewish dietary laws by eating only kosher food. So the Galatians said, "OK, no more ham sandwiches for us." The preachers told them, "You've also got to celebrate the Passover if you really want to belong to God; and then you've got to observe the Sabbath, too. And to help you out, we'll give you a list of things you are not allowed to do on the Sabbath." Then the preachers said, "Oh, and by the way, you have to be circumcised, too." (That's a daunting one!) There were literally hundreds of Jewish religious laws. In short, the Judaizers were trying to get the Galatians to jump on their religious treadmill.

Today we might hear the same kind of teaching, only with a different set of requirements for salvation. The new list might include items like, "Go to church, pray, serve, give. Believe in Jesus and do these religious duties, then God will accept you and you'll be saved."

Still, this is fake good news. Religious duties don't save us. If anyone would know that, it would be the Apostle Paul. In Galatians 1:14 he reminds them, "I was advancing in Judaism beyond many of my own age among my people and was extremely zealous for the traditions of my fathers." Nobody did religion better than Paul. Although it wasn't until he experienced the grace of Jesus that he truly knew God. He later wrote, "For it is by grace you have been saved, through faith—and this is not from yourselves, it is the gift of God— not by works, so that no one can boast" (Ephesians 2:8-9).

Our salvation is a gift of grace from God. We don't earn that gift by doing religious activities, we receive it as a gift through faith in Christ.

There is nothing wrong with trying to do good works. We should worship and serve the poor, but these activities don't save us. We do those things because we have been made right with God, not in order that God will accept us. That's what the very next verse says: "For we are God's handiwork, created in Christ Jesus to do good works, which God prepared in advance for us to do" (Ephesians 2:10).

So, first we are saved by grace, then we do good. Not vice versa. Anytime someone says that to be accepted by God you have to believe and do these other things, you'll know that's fake good news.

Fake Good News: "To be accepted by God, just be sincere in what you believe."

In other words, it doesn't matter what you believe as long as you are sincere about it. This philosophy is based on the idea that all paths lead to God; all religions are equal as long as you truly believe yours. This is also fake good news.

The Judaizers were very sincere in their beliefs. They traveled all the way from Jerusalem to tell the Galatians they needed to adopt Judaism in order to be saved. They meant it. But that does not mean it was true. Terrorists are sincere enough in their beliefs to die for them. That doesn't make them right. A person can be sincere and sincerely wrong at the same time.

We don't invent a truth by the sincerity of our belief. Look at what Paul says in Chapter 1, verses 8 and 9:

> "But even if we or an angel from heaven should preach
> a gospel other than the one we preached to you, let
> them be under God's curse! As we have already said, so now I say
> again: If anybody is preaching to you a gospel other than what you
> accepted, let them be under God's curse!"

Paul was downright impolite when rejecting the Judaizer's sincere belief. The reason Paul became so intense was because he realizes what is at stake when people accept a fake gospel.

Counterfeit drugs are fake medicine. People who take them think they are taking a prescription their doctors ordered, but instead they end up with any number of hidden poisons such as road paint, antifreeze or an undeclared and unapproved medication. For example, in February 2005, a 23-year-old man in Myanmar came down with malaria. Doctors prescribed him artesunate, an inexpensive anti-malaria drug. Typically, a patient recovers after a few days on the drug, but this young man grew much worse. He slipped into a coma and his kidneys started failing. His doctors tried to save him, but they were too late. The infection spread to his brain and killed him. It turns out that the artesunate given to the patient had only 20 percent of the active ingredient required to kill the parasites. It was a fake drug, and it killed him.[62] World police agency Interpol says more than one million people die each year from counterfeit drugs.[63]

I wonder how many people die spiritually each year because of a fake gospel. Even one is a tragedy, and that's why Paul spoke so bluntly and passionately against it.

There is a word for the fake good news that our salvation depends on how well we obey religious and moral rules; it is

---

62 *The Fake Drug Industry is Exploding...* http://www.newsweek.com/2015/09/25/fake-drug-in-dustry-exploding-and-we-cant-do-anything-about-it-373088.html

63 *Insight Crime* http://www.insightcrime.org/news-briefs/counterfeit-drugs-kill-1-million-annual-ly-interpol

called "legalism." This is what the Apostle Paul was trying to help the Galatians avoid. Legalism is wrong because it makes us think that obeying laws is what saves us, not Jesus and the Holy Spirit. If we fall for legalism, like the Galatians did, then we will probably get frustrated and worn out at some point. Worse, we will never really know whether we are right with God.

Real Good News

The true gospel produces results the fake gospel does not. For one, ***through the true gospel we are made alive in Christ.*** Jesus did not come to make bad people good, Jesus came to make dead people live! This happens by God's grace through faith.

In Ephesians 2:4-5, Paul writes, "But because of his great love for us, God, who is rich in mercy, made us alive with Christ even when we were dead in transgressions—it is by grace you have been saved."

Apart from Christ, we have no life; we are "dead in transgressions." Our bodies aren't dead, but our spirits are. The part of us that relates to God had no life. That means that when our bodies die, we will be completely dead forever. No amount of religion or good deeds will change that.

Eight years ago I was at the local gym running on a treadmill when I collapsed with a cardiac arrest. I had no pulse. Fortunately, a doctor who was there working out saw me go down. He used an AED machine to shock my heart back to beating. I had surgery and I feel great today. I have no heart damage and I still run three to four miles most days.

I was literally saved by grace. I was on the floor without a pulse. There was nothing I could do to save myself. I'm so grateful that the doctor didn't stand over me and give me self-improvement tips. I'm glad he didn't say, "Steve, you don't look very good. Eat more vegetables and reduce your stress." No, he didn't tell me what I should do, he stepped in and saved me because I couldn't do anything to save myself. Because he acted, I'm alive and well today.

Apart from Christ, each of us is spiritually dead. It doesn't help if someone says, "You should try to stop getting angry so often" or, "You should serve the homeless once a month." Those are great things to do if you are spiritually alive, but religious activities won't make dead people live. If you take a corpse to church, it is still dead. If you haul it with you on a mission trip, it's just going to stink. We are spiritually dead until Jesus makes alive again by grace. It is only his mercy that makes us alive, and we receive that through faith.

Secondly, *through the true gospel we can know we are accepted by God.*

Some years ago, I was in Latin America when a hurricane was bearing down on the city. Our team was due to leave the next day, but because of the approaching storm we headed to the airport to try to get a flight out immediately. I knew that the airport would be closed in just a matter of hours, and if we didn't get out that day we would be stuck in a hurricane.

When we arrived at the airport there were long lines of people trying to get on one of the few flights out. People with confirmed tickets for that day looked fairly relaxed. The rest of us weren't. We were waiting anxiously, wondering if there would be a seat left by the time we got to the desk. As it turns out, all six of us got on the plane. The rain started to fall as we were taking off. In those situations, there is a big difference between having a confirmed reservation and hoping you get a seat on standby.

One of the great privileges we have as followers of Jesus is the ability to know that we have a confirmed place in heaven. We do not need to live with the uncertainty of someone on standby. We can go from "hoping" to "knowing."

Hebrews 10:22 encourages us,

> "[L]et us draw near to God with a sincere heart and with
> the *full assurance* that faith brings, having our hearts
> sprinkled to cleanse us from a guilty conscience and
> having our bodies washed with pure water."

If we need to be good morally enough to be accepted by God, then we will never have assurance. Religious duties do not give us assurance, either. If sincerity is the requirement for being accepted by God, then we'll always need to be scanning our hearts for any wavering. But through the true gospel of salvation by grace through faith, we can draw near to God with "full assurance that faith brings."

This "assurance" (as in the song "Blessed Assurance") is one of the distinctive teachings of the Wesleyan tradition. John Wesley experienced it when he was converted at the Bible study on Aldersgate Street. He wrote,

> "I felt my heart strangely warmed. I felt I did trust in Christ, Christ alone for salvation, and an ***assurance*** was given me that He had taken my sin, even mine."

Later, Wesley clarified, "The assurance of which I alone speak I should not choose to call an assurance of salvation, but rather (with the Scriptures), the assurance of faith ..."[64] He said that the Holy Spirit can give us the inner assurance that we have put our faith in Christ, and so we know that we are his. That is because God promised that if we believe Jesus rose from the dead and we declare that he is our Lord (leader), then we are saved (Romans 10:9). Our assurance rests on God's promise, not our performance.

We don't need to settle for, "I hope I'm going to heaven ..." In Psalm 23:6 says, "Surely your goodness and love will follow me all the days of my life, and I will dwell in the house of the Lord forever." We can express the same sentiment, because it's not our effort or track record that makes us confident – it is the promise of God that gives us assurance. Once new life is born in us, faith allows us to know it.

---

64 John Wesley letter dated September 28, 1738

Chapter Eleven Discussion Questions
Know it

1. What was the most unforgettable gift you ever received? Gave?

2. Why was the Apostle Paul so forceful in his denunciation of those distorting the Gospel? (Galatians 1:6-7)

3. Which of the following fake Good News statements do you find most believable? In what ways does it differ from the true Gospel (1 Corinthians 15)

To be accepted by God:

- "Be a pretty good person"
- "Believe and be religious"
- "Just be sincere."

4. Why is it not arrogant to say that we are confident we are accepted by God and bound for heaven?

5. How can assurance of our salvation strengthen our faith?

CHAPTER TWELVE
With Heart and Mind

Faith certainly tells us what the senses do not, but not the contrary of what they see; it is above, not against them.

— Blaise Pascal

In August of 1662, Blaise Pascal died at the young age of 39. After his death, his housekeeper was sorting through his clothes and closets when she found a neatly folded piece of paper. It had been sewn into the lining of the jacket Pascal wore every day. Clearly, this paper was so important to him that he wanted it close to him at all times.

Pascal was not just smart; he was brilliant. At age 10 he was doing original experiments in math and science. By the time he was sixteen years old, he had several mathematical break-throughs to his credit and was an accepted member of the professional mathematics community. When he was age nineteen, he invented and sold a mechanical calculator. He discovered a law of hydraulics. Today, a "Pascal" is the name given to a unit of pressure that measures internal pressure and stress. "Pascal's triangle" is an arithmetical triangle used in algebra and probability theory. As I say, he was a brilliant guy.

For most of his life, Pascal was a Christian in name only. His life was shaped primarily by social and scientific pursuits. That all changed on the night of November 23, 1654. Pascal was at home alone. He decided to read an account of the crucifixion of Jesus when he sensed the nearness of Christ in a powerful way.

For the next two hours, he had an overwhelming experience of the presence of the living God. As soon as it was over, he did his best to describe in writing his experience. This is what he wrote:

"The year of grace 1654,

Monday, 23 November, … From about half past ten at night until about half past midnight,

FIRE.

GOD of Abraham, GOD of Isaac, GOD of Jacob
not of the philosophers and of the learned.
Certitude. Certitude. Feeling. Joy. Peace.
GOD of Jesus Christ.
My God and your God.
Your GOD will be my God.
Forgetfulness of the world and of everything, except GOD.
He is only found by the ways taught in the Gospel.
Grandeur of the human soul.
Righteous Father, the world has not known you, but I have known you.
Joy, joy, joy, tears of joy.
I have departed from him:
They have forsaken me, the fount of living water.
My God, will you leave me?
Let me not be separated from him forever.
This is eternal life, that they know you, the one true God, and the one that you sent, Jesus Christ.
Jesus Christ.
Jesus Christ.
I left him; I fled him, renounced, crucified.
Let me never be separated from him.
He is only kept securely by the ways taught in the Gospel:
Renunciation, total and sweet.
Complete submission to Jesus Christ and to my director.
Eternally in joy for a day's exercise on the earth.
May I not forget your words. Amen." [65]

---

65 *A Night of Fire*, https://churchpop.com/2016/04/19/night-fire-blaise-pascals/

No one knew that Pascal kept this written record of his encounter with God in the lining of his coat for the rest of his life. But they did know that something happened to Pascal that made him different. After his mystical experience with God, Pascal focused his considerable intellect toward writing a defense of the faith. Unfortunately, he did not live long enough to complete his work. A draft of his notes was collected and published after his death, which is known today as "Pensées" ("thoughts"). In it, his logical mind appeals to readers to consider Christ on the basis of reason. At the same time, he also acknowledges the limits of reason when it comes to leading us to Jesus. He wrote, "The heart has its reasons which reason knows nothing of. ... We know the truth not only by the reason, but by the heart."

Both Heart and Mind

Both the mind and the heart play an important role in the development of our faith. Pascal was jolted out of a doubting indifference and into a passionate confidence in Christ by an intense encounter with the living God. One might assume that someone as intellectually gifted as Pascal would first have required compelling reasons to trust Christ. Instead, Jesus entered his life through the doorway of a mystical encounter. Yet, as soon as Pascal experienced the reality of God's love, he set about using his mind to try to convince others that faith in Christ was rational.

Faith involves both our heart and our mind. In Matthew 22:37 Jesus said that the greatest commandment is, "'Love the Lord your God with all your *heart* and with all your *soul* and with all your *mind.*'".

Having faith does not mean living exclusively out of our emotions and pretending that we have no brain. Neither does it consist only of thinking correct theological thoughts and steering clear of emotional experiences. We need both heart and mind. If we do not engage both, our faith may weaken unnecessarily over the long haul. A rational foundation for our faith will enable it to withstand exposure to the rigors of life, and experiencing the refreshing personal touch of God's Spirit gives us the confidence and motivation to obey God's words. We are called to love God with our whole being – mind, body and soul.

Each of us takes our own path toward spiritual maturity. For some of us, our faith is born when our minds grasp the truth of the Gospel, and later it is ignited by experiences of God that touch our heart. Thomas Aquinas is one such historical example.

Aquinas was born in 1224 and is one of the towering figures of Christian scholarship. He is considered a saint by the Roman Catholic Church. Many regard him as the epitome of a teacher of theology. Aquinas wrote over 100 books. He worked for twenty years on his crowning achievement: *Summa Theologica*. It was a brilliant work that blended Greek philosophy with Christian theology and shaped the thinking of western thought for centuries to come.

Thomas' writing came to an abrupt end one night in 1273. He was celebrating mass when he had a vision from God that profoundly impacted him. He said, "The end of my labors has come. All that I have written appears to be as so much straw after the things that have been revealed to me." When later asked to return to writing, Aquinas said, "I can write no more. I have seen things that make my writings like straw."[66]

Whatever Thomas saw was so awe-inducing that he felt that any words he would write could never adequately express the reality of God's glory he glimpsed. Even so, Thomas' work was not mere straw. His ideas influenced literally millions of Christians over the centuries. Thomas first trusted and obeyed God primarily with his mind. Later, a personal experience of God's presence enriched his faith.

For other believers, it is the other way around. Faith begins when their hearts are touched by God's Spirit, then it is developed with their minds. John Wesley is one case in point.

John Wesley sought to know God personally for years. Finally, God met him at a meeting on Aldersgate Street. He

---

66 *When St. Thomas Aquinas likened his work to straw, was that a retraction of what he wrote? By Peggy Frye* https://www.catholic.com/index.php/qa/when-st-thomas-aquinas-likened-his-work-to-straw-was-that-a-retraction-of-what-he-wrote

famously declared, "I felt my heart strangely warmed." Wesley also had a powerful experience of God's presence a few months later at a different prayer meeting. He describes what happened in his journal entry dated January 1, 1739:

> "Mr. Hall, Hinching, Ingham, Whitefield, Hutching, and my brother Charles were present at our love feast in Fetter Lane with about 60 of our brethren. About three in the morning, as we were continuing instant in prayer, the power of God came mightily upon us insomuch that many cried out for exceeding joy and many fell to the ground. As soon as we were recovered a little from that awe and amazement at the presence of His majesty, we broke out with one voice, 'We praise Thee, O God, we acknowledge Thee to be the Lord.'"

These encounters with God's presence helped launch Wesley's faith. He went on to become the leader of a powerful revival movement that swept through England and resulted in the birth of the Methodist Church.

Wesley's faith began with a touch of God's Spirit, yet it did not exclude his mind. In the decades following his conversion, Wesley put his considerable intellect to work. He wrote or edited over 400 publications. He guided the development of the Methodist movement through his teaching. He also wrote about music, medicine, slavery and even politics. The faith that began in his "strangely warmed" heart also included his mind.

Historian Henry Rack titled his definitive biography of Wesley, *Reasonable Enthusiast*,[67] capturing the Methodist leader's embrace of both heart and mind. In the eighteenth century, the staid Church of England clergy labeled the early Methodists "enthusiasts" because emotional expressions were common in Methodist meetings. At the same time, Wesley was also called "reasonable" because of his detailed teaching and rational defense of the movement.

Although both heart and mind are vital to growing in our faith, by nature most of us favor one or the other. Yet, developing

---

67 *Reasonable Enthusiast,* by Henry Rack, Epworth Press; 3rd edition (Peterborough, England) 2014

HEAR IT · SEE IT · RISK IT

the aspect of faith that comes less naturally can create a growth
opportunity for us. If you are most accustomed to relating to God
through your study and teaching, you can grow in fresh ways
by inviting the Holy Spirit to touch your heart. And if you are
already accustomed to experiencing God's presence that way,
you can grow by strengthening your grip on the rationale for
your faith.

Opening the Heart

Experiences of God's presence provide moments of spiritual
refreshing. Encountering God's presence strengthens our faith
because we see God for who he is. We recognize his holiness,
power and goodness. That prompts us to trust him more. After
all, we trust people we have met more readily than those we only
heard of in third-person stories. Faith in God is fundamentally
personal because it consists of trusting a person (Jesus), not an
idea. We obey the direction of a personal God; we do not obey an
abstract concept.

I have never had an experience with God that was as intense
as Blaise Pascal's, but God has touched my heart numerous
times in less dramatic ways. In my periods of greatest stress and
pain, I have recognized the Holy Spirit's whisper, reassuring
me that he was present. There have been times in worship when
God's holiness has overwhelmed me. At other times, his love
has filled my soul, giving me courage and strength. I have been
enveloped in profound peace while alone with Jesus in prayer.
These experiences of God's presence fanned the flame of my love
for Jesus. And yes, they strengthened my faith.

Perhaps you, too, could name a number of times God has
personally touched your life. Cherish and enjoy those moments,
but do not depend on them as the only way to grow your faith. We
cannot summon or manufacture these kinds of experiences. It is
not spiritually healthy to chase them. We don't grow in faith by
waiting for a divine encounter to fall upon us. But we can invite
them and remain open them whenever God chooses to connect
with us in this way. Here are some ways we can open our hearts
to a touch from God:

Invite God's Touch Through Prayer

Prayer is communion with God. We speak and we listen. At other times we quietly enjoy Jesus' company. We are more likely to hear the whisper of God's voice when we take the time to listen for it. We are more likely to sense his presence when we are still before him than when we are dashing to an appointment.

To make our hearts available to God's Spirit, spend time with him. The Psalmists wrote (and sang) about seeking God. Pascal, Aquinas and Wesley all encountered God while they were seeking him. Pascal was alone, Aquinas was celebrating the Eucharist in public worship, and Wesley was at informal small group gatherings.

Seek God in prayer, letting him know you desire more of him. Pray with the Psalmist, "As the deer pants for streams of water, so my soul pants for you, my God."[68]

Spend Time with People Who Experience God

It is encouraging and inspiring to talk with people who have experienced God in personal ways. It can also stir expectation within us. We sense that if it happened to them, it can happen to us. When we spend time with others, we pick up their perspective and way of thinking. That opens us up to new ways of encountering God.

If you don't know many people who have experienced God in significant ways, don't despair. One way to spend time with people of faith that we will never meet is to read their stories. There are many good memoirs and devotional classics by Christians from the past that can encourage us to press into God ourselves.

Worship Wholeheartedly

Worshiping God privately and publicly opens us to his presence. If you worship God primarily with your mind, try intentionally involving your heart. To make our hearts available to

---

68 Psalm 42:1

him, include words denoting emotion in your praise. Like the Psalmist,

> "Shout for joy to God, all the earth!
> Sing the glory of His name;
> make his praise glorious." [69]

Try engaging your whole being. Use your physical posture to praise God by lifting hands or bowing before him. If this is not comfortable or common for you, it is an opportunity for growth.

Developing Your Mind

Of course, we do not need to become mystics in order to live by faith. You may always be a "head-first" believer, and that is perfectly fine! That may be the way God has wired you. However, that does not mean you cannot also experience God's personal touch. Jesus told us to love him with our hearts and minds.

I grew up in a logical family. My father was an engineer for nuclear power plants. My brother is a physics teacher and pursued a Ph.D. in engineering. I grew up in an environment that valued clear thinking and rational explanations. So, after I came to faith in Christ, it didn't take long for me to start asking questions.

The reality of God cannot be "proven," but it is not irrational. Faith is not another name for logical inconsistencies. God created a universe of order. He created us with minds and expects us to use them.

Some Christians have developed a suspicion or even hostility to learning. That is tragic. Many of the world's greatest intellects and scientists have been followers of Jesus. There is no conflict between faith and science, trust and knowledge.

As we saw in an earlier chapter, doubt is a question. If we try to ignore our questions, they fester and undermine our ability to trust and obey God's words. On the other hand, our faith grows when we resolve our questions because we are more confident in

---

69 Psalm 66:1-2

acting on what God tells us. I offered suggestions on dealing with the faith questions in chapter six. Of course, we will never have all the answers to every question this side of heaven. Life and faith include mystery. But remember, if you have a question, it has been asked before.

Loving God with our minds goes beyond just answering doubt-inducing questions. It also includes building on our understanding of what we believe. Here are some ways to do that:

Learn More About Scripture

Reading the Scripture is an essential way to feed our faith. The more we know about the Bible, the more we will be able to get out of reading it. Understanding the context and culture of a book of the Bible will help us understand what God is saying to us. And then we will be able to respond more faithfully.

For example, when we know about the history of the Jews' conflict with the Samaritan people, Jesus' point in the parable of the Good Samaritan becomes much more vivid. It helps to know why the Jews considered the Samaritans to be traitors and a threat to their future, and that they were convinced that it pleased God for them to have nothing to do with the Samaritans.

We can learn about the world of the Bible from commentaries, which are books written by scholars who provide the background and detailed interpretations of each book of the Bible. Bible encyclopedias and Bible dictionaries offer valuable insight into concepts, people and events. Some of these resources are available online.

Faith is hearing and responding to God's word. The more accurately we understand the Scripture's message, the better we will be able to respond to what God is really saying to us. That will keep us from misunderstandings which can weaken our faith.

Explore Theological Concepts

"Theology" sounds like a complicated and intimidating subject best left to the experts. Actually, theology simply refers to thoughts about God and religion. Everyone has ideas about what God is like, so that makes everyone a theologian of sorts. Our ideas are important because they determine how we respond to God.

Let's imagine, for example, a young mother's infant son dies from a congenital heart defect. If she believes that God killed her son, she may turn away from him in anger and grief. On the other hand, if she believes that her son died because we live in a fallen world that God is redeeming, she may turn toward God for strength and healing in her grief. The difference is in her theology of pain – in other words, what she believes about God's role in pain.

We love God with our minds and strengthen our faith by developing informed understandings of topics such as how prayer works, the nature of sin, salvation and more. What we believe about these issues affects our ability to trust and respond to God's words to us, so it is worth investing time and energy to go to a class, read a book, watch a video or even enroll in school.

Learn About the History of the Church

We are not the first people to follow Christ. There have been 2,000 years of history before us. We do well to learn from the experience of the church fathers and mothers. They can instruct us in matters such as how to live in a culture that doesn't honor God, or how to respond when the church loses its way morally. We gain a better understanding of God's purposes when we learn about how the church developed out of Old Testament roots, through its birth on the day of Pentecost and through the centuries until today.

"There is nothing new under the sun." Whatever we are facing today has a precedent. We need to be very careful about adopting a stance or a teaching that is completely new, as if no one was ever holy enough or smart enough to think of it until we did. If we are going to respond to God's word to us it really helps to see how others did so over the centuries.

Growing in faith means responding to God with our whole

being. That includes heart and mind. The more of ourselves we offer to God, the more of his life we receive.

Chapter Twelve Discussion Questions
With Heart and Mind

1. Do you cry at movies?

2. Why is it essential to love God with both our hearts and our minds?

3. Each of us tend to favor one over the other. Which way do you most naturally nurture your relationship with God - with your heart or your mind? How so?

4. What component could you add to your worship experience in order to strengthen the side of faith that is least natural to you?

5. What is God saying to you about growing in your faith? What will you do about it?

Conclusion

"We live by faith, not by sight."

2 Corinthians 5:7

Your faith can grow. I hope you are convinced of that! No matter what your faith level is today, it can grow. Hear it, see it and risk it. Then repeat. The more your faith increases, the more of God's goodness you will taste.

1 Corinthians 2:9 tells us, "'What no eye has *seen,* what no ear has *heard,* and what no human mind has *conceived*'— the things God has prepared for those who love him."

No matter what you have heard, there is more. No matter what you have seen – "you ain't seen nothin' yet." And the next step of faith you risk can release more of God's blessing than you think possible.

In the end, we are not seeking faith, we are seeking Jesus. Our goal is not to attain a spiritual state we label "faith," our goal is to know Jesus. That includes being close enough to him to hear him speak. To know Jesus deeply is to trust him deeply.

As you take steps to grow in your faith, be patient with yourself. God is. He knows it takes time for trust to grow. New patterns of thinking don't take root overnight. Habits take months to become second nature. We will risk steps of obedience and celebrate thrilling victories. But we will also stumble into episodes of doubt, fear and sin. Sometimes, too, life's routine will be so ordinary that we won't discern anything happening. God loves us all the time. No matter how you would describe your faith level today, God loves you deeply. Faith is a journey, not a destination. Enjoy the trip.

Acknowledgements

Every book is a team effort.

I want to express my gratitude to my wife, who encouraged me and put up with my writing during my off hours that I normally would have spent with her. I love you and couldn't do it without you!

Thank you to my publisher, Kevin Slimp, my editor, Kristin Lighter, and the team at Market Square Books, who responded immediately and enthusiastically to the idea of working together to publish this book.

A big thank you to Cheryl Berresford, for tirelessly proof-reading and correcting my typos. Someday I will master the use of the comma, or maybe not.

Thanks to Dave Ferguson for suggesting the title.

My intercessory prayer team interceded for me to finish this book – another prayer answered!

And a huge thank you to the people of Crossroads Church, who model what it means to live by faith.

Grow Your Faith

with these books from Market Square

marketsquarebooks.com

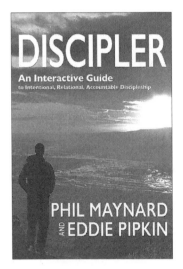

Discipler

Phil Maynard & Eddie Pipkin

Hear It, See It, Risk It

Steve Cordle

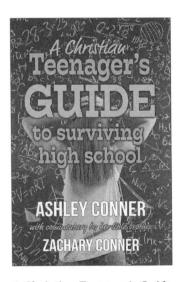

A Christian Teenager's Guide to Surviving High School

Ashley Conner

IMPACT!

Reclaiming the Call of Lay Ministry

Kay Kotan & Blake Bradford

Grow Your Faith

with these books from Market Square

marketsquarebooks.com

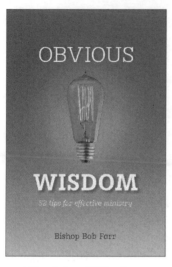

Obvious Wisdom

Bishop Bob Farr

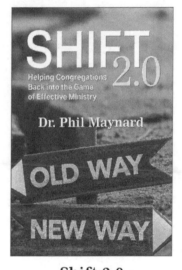

Shift 2.0

Phil Maynard

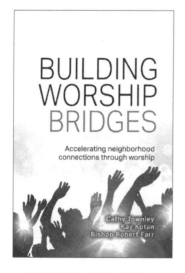

Building Worship Bridges

Cathy Townley

Get Out of that Box!

Anne Bosarge

Made in the USA
Columbia, SC
07 April 2019